皆大欢喜

As You Like It
Catching up in an age of Global English

Samuel Jones
Peter Bradwell

DEM⊙S

DEM⊕S

About Demos

Who we are
Demos is the think tank for everyday democracy. We believe everyone should be able to make personal choices in their daily lives that contribute to the common good. Our aim is to put this democratic idea into practice by working with organisations in ways that make them more effective and legitimate.

What we work on
We focus on six areas: public services; science and technology; cities and public space; people and communities; arts and culture; and global security.

Who we work with
Our partners include policy-makers, companies, public service providers and social entrepreneurs. Demos is not linked to any party but we work with politicians across political divides. Our international network – which extends across Eastern Europe, Scandinavia, Australia, Brazil, India and China – provides a global perspective and enables us to work across borders.

How we work
Demos knows the importance of learning from experience. We test and improve our ideas in practice by working with people who can make change happen. Our collaborative approach means that our partners share in the creation and ownership of new ideas.

What we offer
We analyse social and political change, which we connect to innovation and learning in organisations. We help our partners show thought leadership and respond to emerging policy challenges.

How we communicate
As an independent voice, we can create debates that lead to real change. We use the media, public events, workshops and publications to communicate our ideas. All our books can be downloaded free from the Demos website.

www.demos.co.uk

2007

© Demos

Some rights reserved – see copyright licence for details

ISBN 10 digit: 1-84180-178-X
ISBN 13 digit: 978-1-84180-178-0
Copy edited by Julie Pickard, London
Typeset by utimestwo, Collingtree, Northants
Printed by IPrint, Leicester

For further information and
subscription details please contact:

Demos
Magdalen House
136 Tooley Street
London SE1 2TU

telephone: 0845 458 5949
email: hello@demos.co.uk
web: www.demos.co.uk

Language is the armoury of the human mind; and at once contains the trophies of the past and the weapons of the future.

Samuel Taylor Coleridge[1]

Contents

Acknowledgements

We would like initially to thank the many people to whom we have spoken in the course of researching this pamphlet. In particular, though, we would like to mention David Graddol, whose thoughts during the research were very helpful. His whose pamphlet *English Next*, which seeks to examine how policy might be shaped in response to many of the trends that he has observed, was a vital starting point for this work. Also, thanks must go to Joseph Lo Bianco who shared his thoughts and writing with us from Australia.

In China, Mickey Bonin and He Meizi were kind with both their time and their hospitality. The expertise of Bene't Steinberg and Nick Saville were vital in fincssing the text. As always, our colleagues at Demos have been supportive and insightful in their comments. We would like to thank, in alphabetical order, Kirsten Bound, Rachel Briggs, Charlie Edwards, Catherine Fieschi, John Holden, Duncan O'Leary, Jack Stilgoe, Molly Webb and Shelagh Wright. Thanks also to Peter Harrington for his help in seeing the pamphlet through to publication.

Thanks also to the Demos interns who helped support the project. Again, in alphabetical order, they are Margaret Bolter, Iason Gabriel, Robert Harding, Alyssa Joye, Steven Skelton and Simeon Williams. As ever, all errors and omissions remain our own.

Samuel Jones and Peter Bradwell
March 2007

Executive summary

The English language is spoken the world over. Tourists and business people can travel from native English-speaking countries and be confident that, wherever they go, someone will speak English. Nearly two-thirds of the world's top companies are from Anglophone countries. English is the operating language of over 80 per cent of international organisations. The dominance of US brands, in particular, carry and reinforce the language around the world.

The dominance of English brings its native speakers many advantages. The US, the world's most powerful country, speaks English: when Thomas Jefferson wrote the Declaration of Independence, he did it in English. For the UK, the historical home of English, its global prevalence brings great benefit. One estimate is that, by virtue of being the world's common language, the English language is worth an extra £14.5 billion to the UK economy. In science, the majority of texts are published in English and English-speaking scientists have much easier access to publication and information than scientists who work only in other tongues. Moreover, the English language plays a significant part in attracting professionals and students from all over the world to work in the UK. Institutions like the BBC and the universities are central to maintaining the UK's currency and attraction as the home of the world's language.

The downside of this advantage is that we – the UK and its citizens

– have rested too easily on our laurels. We have retained ways of thinking about the English language that were more suited to empire than they are to a modern, globalised world and we are at risk of becoming outdated. With the dominance of English, we have failed to concentrate sufficiently on learning other languages and we miss out on the opportunities that they open. And, at the same time, speakers of those other languages are becoming ever more proficient in using English and will be better positioned to operate multilingually in a globalised world.

However, at the same time changes in power have led to changes in languages. Other languages, like Mandarin, Urdu, Portuguese and Spanish, are likely to rise in influence and reflect the growing power of China, India and South America. Now, there could be about 1.3 billion speakers of English, and only about 330 million of those native. This is the reality of global English. The overwhelming majority of speakers are non-native, and as people bring with them different cultures and contexts, and different experiences of using English, so the language itself has changed. English is now more a language family than a single language with different forms appearing such as 'Chinglish', 'Hinglish' and 'Singlish'.

Many of the assumptions that we have of English are rooted in outdated worldviews. We need to recognise that English is no longer the language of Empire and that its capitalist and commercial dominance can be both a hindrance and a boon. This is as much about taking the opportunities that global English offers as it is about changing our outlook. Where we once directed the spread of English around the world, we are now just one of many shareholders in the asset that it represents.

As You Like It argues that all these changes create a new agenda for government. English plays a central role in different areas and contexts, so it must come to the fore of policy thinking in all these areas. **All government departments should develop a language strategy to look at the importance of changes in global English and the growth of other languages in their areas of concern.** In line with this, and as it is used for different purposes around the world, **English**

language provision should meet the needs of learners in specific areas and in terms that concentrate on communicative ability, rather than fulfilling demands that others have of them.

As You Like It sets out a programme for change. We must respond to the changes that global English represents in ways that fit with its use around the world. This entails an approach by government that is on occasion directive, and on occasion more sensitive to the free market and democratic forces that English now encompasses.

○ *Responding to individual interest in the way that English is used:* As people learn English as a language of opportunity more than as a way of fitting in with UK or US power, we must teach learners according to their personal and particular interests. In the UK, we must teach learners skills of integration – basic, functional language skills – and the skills to contribute their own experiences.

○ *Responding to the market forces that English represents:* English is a global resource that we must learn to use; we should develop a series of 'English language ambassadors' from specific fields; the government could build on this appeal to create links around the world.

○ *Responding to the need for a common medium of communication:* The prevalence of English gives us the opportunity to develop *cultural literacy* and the skills to accommodate and identify the different perspectives that they bring; we need to use new technologies and common communication to give opportunities to young people and others to take part in a global conversation with their English-speaking peers from around the world.

○ *Taking directive action where appropriate:* Although the choice to use or learn English is a preference and can no longer be used as an expression of one nation's power, there are occasions in which the UK government could and should take action. In part, this must entail motivating the learning of other languages. Recommendations include starting language lessons early and building motivation to study languages, developing the skills of UK schoolchildren in accommodating to different forms of English. Action must also include use of the English language to open opportunity to learners in developing contexts.

○ Also, London and the UK have the chance to *use the 2012 Olympics to develop skills in language and accommodation and to demonstrate an understanding of the UK's new position in the world:* a multilingual Olympiad would be a vital step in redressing the impact of the Anglophone image that the UK can have overseas, such as that expressed by the foreign ambassadors to the UK mentioned in this pamphlet.

1. From 1707 to 2007
The English language and power

Outside St Paul's Cathedral stands a statue of Queen Anne. At her feet are the four continents of Africa, America, Asia and Europe. In 1707, the new Britain looked forward to an imperial future. Over the coming centuries, the dominion of Anne and her successors was to stretch from the novel grid system of the streets of William Penn's new town, Pennsylvania, to the imposing colonial façades of Shanghai's Bund. All over the world, the royal crest came to represent power.

In 2007, three centuries after the Act of Union in which it was formed, Britain is in an age of transition. There is no empire and there is no dominion. The royal crest has given way to the crossed boxes of democracy. However, one thing remains. It bound the Empire more tightly than any garter or sash of court. Where the British themselves have long gone, and British authority has dissipated, the English language has thrived. Its story is about shifts in power. Further shifts and new voices that are emerging will shape its future.

The English language is 'perhaps the most important single export of the last 300 years'.[2] Now, it is used by between 600 million and one billion people across the world. 'Use' is the important word. People don't just speak languages; they use them for their many different purposes. English is changing as it is fitted to new contexts by new people. New words are coined to meet new needs, and influences have come in from other languages.

In the UK, being native speakers of what has become the world's language, we have access to markets, we can travel and communicate easily and speakers of other languages come here to learn and develop their English skills. Partly because the language is now global and no longer so directly associated with imposed authority, people adopt it more as a tool than as a requirement. The UK also has the advantage of sharing our language with the world's most powerful nation and the origin of much of the world's commerce, the US. However, as much as this brings dollars and influence, it also prompts resentment and hostility.

Whichever way we look at it, English is vital to the UK's success. It is bound so closely to power and advantage that speakers of other languages are rapidly developing greater proficiency in its use. Beijing, the host of the 2008 Olympics, has launched a major campaign to develop its citizens' skills in English prior to the arrival of the world's sports people, media, tourists and money. In India, there may be as many as 350 million people using the language.

English is also vital to specific domains and professions. The overwhelming majority of science and technology publications are in English; as a result, we have easy access to innovation from around the world. Furthermore, such benefit extends beyond specific areas. We can read menus in English pretty much anywhere and, when we travel to China, India or elsewhere, we can keep up to date with events in English-language newspapers. Sitting at home, we can type English words into search engines and access material of which our imperial predecessors could not dream.

The problem is that, with this advantage at our fingertips, we do not stop to think what is going on and being discussed in other languages and in different forms of English. Rarely do we wonder what might happen if speaking English stopped being such an advantage. Around the world, people use English in ways that fit their purposes and their needs. English is no longer associated solely with native-speaking nations, but with a global community. As a result, it is changing and different forms of English have developed in different contexts.

The linguistic changes that have come about because of this reflect how the world itself is changing. The real story here is about global power and the relationships that English language use represents. Fundamentally the story of English is about the impact and implications of an increasingly connected world and the enmeshed networks of people, information and capital that stretch across borders and between nations.

Where we ran an empire using English, now it enables us to participate in a globalised world. We must develop ways of taking advantage of the opportunities that English offers that better suit the world to which it has become central. It facilitated power, opportunity, influence and reach; but in the UK, counterintuitively, we must learn that where we once directed the spread of English around the world, we are now just one of many shareholders in the asset that it represents.

However, we have made few steps to address this situation. Our attitude to our native tongue stems ultimately from the days of Empire. In an age of globalisation, this is unsustainable. Even with recent policy developments, such as offering languages like Urdu and Mandarin in schools, there has been little government response to the changes that the world has seen. This is a worrying situation. In terms of the English language, a scan of policy across all departments reveals that the two main areas of interest are in selling teaching overseas and as a fairly instrumental requirement for citizenship in the UK. The paucity of the government's policy reflects how much, as a whole, we have missed the significance of the changing relationship between the English language and influence in a globalised world.

For the UK, this creates a threefold problem:

O   We have retained ways of thinking about the English language that were more suited to Empire than they are to the modern, globalised world and we are at risk of becoming outdated and possibly resented.

O   With the dominance of English, our linguistic skills have become impoverished, and we miss out on many of the opportunities that other languages open.

O   At the same time, speakers of those other languages are becoming ever more proficient in using English and will be better positioned to operate multilingually in a globalised world.

The UK and its government need to recognise that the English language of Google and Wikipedia is simply not the English language of Queen Anne and William Penn. As Britain shapes up for the future, the English language and the way that we approach it will be vital to our policy thinking. Today, Anglophone does not mean either British, American or any other native-speaker status: we need to enable our citizens to operate as citizens of a global world.

2. English goes global

As of November 2006, there were 6912 living languages in the world spoken by a total of about six billion people.[3] Variously, scholars and academics have estimated that there are perhaps 500 million speakers of English,[4] or maybe even 800 million.[5] At the moment, though, English ranks only second among the world's most spoken languages.[6] Figure 1 shows an estimate by the linguist Nicholas Ostler of the numbers of people speaking different languages around the world.

This seems at odds with the apparent dominance of English. The difference is that, although not everybody speaks English, it is used in common between speakers whose native languages are different. In linguistics, this is termed a lingua franca.[7] We are living in an age in which English has grown to become the world's lingua franca.

However, even allowing for the many other people in different countries – like India, Jamaica or South Africa – who speak varieties of English, the total figure of native speakers is a good way off the estimated total numbers of English speakers around the world, certainly in relation to the estimate of 800 million speakers. So who are these other speakers? As Ostler says, to account for them we have to factor in second-language speakers 'since it is they who have dominated expansion of English use in the twentieth century'.[8] So, although the number of Mandarin speakers is greater than that of English, the difference comes in *the contexts in which English is used*.

Figure 1 The world's top 20 languages

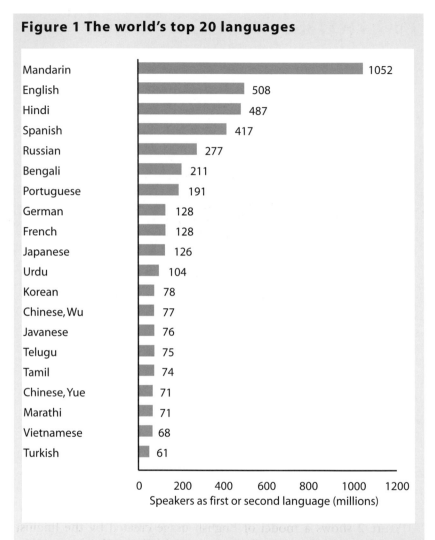

Speakers as first or second language (millions)

Source: N Ostler, *Empires of the Word: A language history of the world* (London: Harper Collins, 2006)

Figure 2 Kachru's model of English around the world

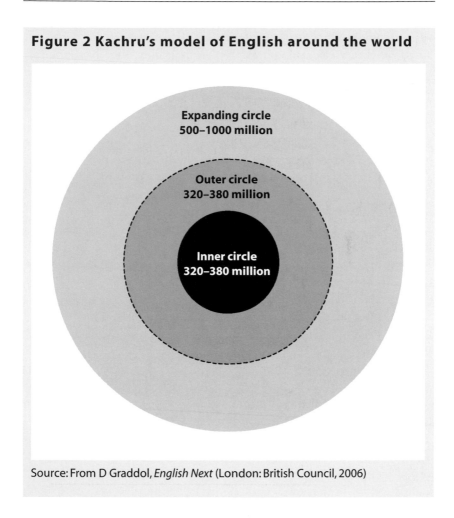

Source: From D Graddol, *English Next* (London: British Council, 2006)

Figure 2 shows a model of English usage created by the linguist Braj Kachru.[9] It is based on the relation of English spoken around the world to a core of native speakers.

The **inner circle** represents countries in which the native tongue is English; it includes countries such as the US, the UK, Australia, Ireland and New Zealand. This is surrounded by the **outer circle**, which comprises countries where English is spoken as a second language, such as Denmark, Finland, India, the Netherlands, Singapore and at least another 50 countries.[10] The **expanding circle** represents countries in which English is learned as a foreign language (EFL); it includes countries like China, Japan, Korea, Russia and a large number of other nations.

Numerically, the balance of power has shifted dramatically to the outer circles. The numbers are notoriously difficult to pin down but, according to one expert, 'where there are currently about 330 million *native* speakers of English, there could be as many as a further 1.3 billion speaking it in very different contexts around the world'.[11] David Graddol, another linguist, suggests that 'within the space of a few years, there could be around two billion people learning English in many different contexts'.[12] This mass uptake will impact heavily on the position of native English speakers in the major English-speaking countries.

This is the shape of English as it is spoken and used in the world today. It has come to unite peoples and cultures from entirely different parts of the world. An example of this came on 15 November 2006, when the Arabic broadcaster, al-Jazeera, launched an English-language news channel. Its managers announced that it would be available in 80 million homes worldwide, providing a 'bridge between cultures' and 'bringing the South to the North'.[13] al-Jazeera is broadcast primarily for English-speaking Arabs from around the world, but it also hopes to have more general appeal. Broadcasting in English represents a major step for the Doha-based station. With a heritage that is overwhelmingly Arabic, it also demonstrates just how global and accessible the English language now is. The example of al-Jazeera tells a wider story. Rather than being associated simply with the interests of native speakers, English is now a language of global opportunity. As we turn to look at how it came to be so, it will become clear that this was not always the case.

The trophies of the past: the association of English and power

Kachru's model helps us understand how English has developed to become a global language in numerical and geographic terms. However, it does not tell the full story. The rise of English is explained ultimately by historical forces and more human motives, and these are central to understanding how it is likely to develop in the future, and how closely it is associated with global power.

People learn English because it is a route into communities that span from business to blogs, from brands to Britpop and from Birmingham to Beijing. Even Latin, the language of another great empire of the past, was spoken only in official contexts across the conquered parts of the then known world and did not present such an image of community. Subsequently, it maintained influence, albeit dwindling, through the establishment power of scholarship and the Catholic Church, both communities in their own right, but speaking in closed terms and as communities of authority. English is different because, throughout its history, it has been adopted to voice different sorts of power.

From the beginnings of the printing press, English benefited from being the language of choice for some of the most diverse forces the world has ever seen: the British Empire, American expansion, capitalism, globalisation and the development of the internet. It is not just that these powers found their voice English, it is that power itself was and is communicated through language.

The historian Niall Ferguson has described how this power has changed:

> The paradox of globalisation is that as the world becomes more integrated, so power becomes more diffuse. Thanks to the dynamism of international capitalism, all but the poorest people in the world have significantly more purchasing power than their grandfathers dared dream of. The means of production were never more productive or – as China and India achieve

their belated economic takeoffs – more widely shared . . . more
people than ever can harness their own brainpower. All these
changes mean that the old monopolies on which power was
traditionally based – monopolies on wealth, political office and
knowledge – have in large measure broken up.[14]

Ferguson wrote primarily of governmental power; he might as well
have been writing about the English language. The shift from
monopoly to globalisation is also the story of power in relation to
English usage. Ferguson continues:

Power, let us not forget, is not just about being able to buy
whatever you want; that is mere wealth. Power is about being
able to get whatever you want at below a market price. It is
about being able to get people to perform services or part with
goods that they would not ordinarily be able to sell at any price.
For empires, those ambitious states that seek to exert power
beyond their own borders, power depends on both the resolve of
the masters and the consent of the subject.[15]

Power, once driven by authority, is now governed by market forces. As
the English language has become a vehicle of globalisation, so the
power that it communicates has been renegotiated between the
authorities of the past, and the users of today and tomorrow. Its story
is one of the shift of power from the few to the many.

Authority: the few to the many

English has been associated with authority since the legal documents
of Anglo-Norman England. Later, a modern standardised English
began to take shape: from the time of William Caxton, English
became more regular and more standardised. As the linguist David
Crystal puts it: 'A standard can evolve without printing; but printing
makes it spread more rapidly and widely. And once the standard is in
the hands of the printers, they do not let it go.'[16] Caxton's press was in
Westminster, as near as possible to the court and power. The

efficiency of printing and the administrative needs of government coincided happily in the English language, and Caxton's choices in stylistic and orthographic matters are reflected in Chancery documents of the day. As we shall see, Caxton's rule of thumb, that 'the common terms that are used daily are more easily understood than old and ancient English', might serve as a useful lesson for the future.[17]

English was not the only language to benefit from the printing press. Invented in Mainz around 1453, the Gutenberg Press is as famous as those of Caxton (1476) and his English successors. Religious reformers, in particular, made use of the new communications technology. Translations of the Bible used the vernacular to represent the words of experts and authority more widely, giving people the power to understand, rather than be told. Later, in the Enlightenment, French, German and English especially were used to challenge the academic and religious supremacy of Latin. These languages also marginalised existing authorities, and communicated new authority. Language came to be a means of questioning the divine origins of the world: new ideas about language growth suggested diversity. This undermined beliefs in the prior uniformity of language and so struck the very heart of the Babel myth. Travelling the world, bringing back foreigners, like the Polynesian, Omai, Western societies encountered languages so very different from their own that concepts of linguistic origin were inverted. Vernacular languages gave thought and philosophy a worldlier, less religious edge. Power was renegotiated through language. In the shift from the Vatican to the vernacular, and the Vulgate to Voltaire, languages played an instrumental role. Nevertheless, while power shifted, the mindset in which knowledge was the dominion of the few remained.

The state to the many

With the discovery of new lands and the drive to colonise, language came to play an even more important and global role. From domestic administrative needs, the imperial powers of Europe had learned the importance of a standardised language. As the need to communicate authority more efficiently grew, what had previously been a distinctly European issue came to bear on the world stage.

The growth of British power and the demands of running an empire meant that English spread. Before the East India Company could bring back tea and other commodities, they had first – even in the most rudimentary form – to export English. Consequently, the Company's eighteenth-century tussle with France for control of the east Asian trade proved significant in the subsequent dominance of English as a world language. In India, wrestling administration from the Mughal Empire laid the foundations for the influence of English that continues to this day. However, as the linguistic interest of company figures like Sir William Jones and the later much-maligned Warren Hastings reveals, this influence was not incompatible with a respect for indigenous tongues and traditions.

English was also one of the means by which the power differences of old Europe came to be resolved. In the New World of America, both religious and secular forces found a virgin land. It provided a perfect setting to start afresh. In religious terms, Protestants saw a chance to establish a new Church. Tom Paine, Thomas Jefferson and, later, Alexis de Tocqueville, saw the chance to mould a new, pure democracy. English had a large part to play in this story, bringing into communion the religious and the secular.

However, as Crystal says, with the discovery, independence and rise of America the pragmatic reasons behind the growth of English continued. These include:

> the expansion of British colonial power, which peaked towards the end of the nineteenth century, and the emergence of the United States as the leading economic power of the twentieth century. It is the latter factor which continues to explain the world position of English today. . . . The USA has nearly 70 per cent of all English mother-tongue speakers in the world. . . . Such dominance, with its political/economic underpinnings, currently gives America a controlling interest in the way the language is likely to develop.[18]

In settling America, colonists had to find new ways of describing the world that they encountered. They either invented new words, or assimilated descriptions they picked up from Native Americans, words like *racoon* and *totem*.[19] A moment of real importance came in the summer of 1776 when Jefferson and his colleagues wrote the Declaration of Independence not in French or German, but in English. In arguing their terms with the motherland, they were securing the future of the mother tongue. A couple of years on, in 1780, one of the signatories, John Adams, proposed the idea of an American Academy to the infant Congress of America. In so doing, he argued that 'English is destined to be in the next and succeeding centuries more generally the language of the world than Latin was in the last or French is in the present age'.[20] As he worked towards his presidency, he could neither have spoken a truer nor a more portentous word.

The twin forces of the British Empire and American growth meant that English was the language both of the old power and the power that was to grow. It had also become the language of scholarship and political innovation; more than that, it had become the language most closely associated with success.

Commerce and capitalism: the market and private companies to the many

With the rise of a more global economy in the twentieth century, English changed from being a language of imperium to being a language of business and commerce. When asked what was likely to be the most influential factor that would determine the course of world politics, Otto von Bismarck remarked that it would be 'the fact that the North Americans speak English'.[21] Like those of Adams, his words have rung true: America's influence has been felt as much in its guns and steel as its brands and companies.

English dominates the world as we experience it. Wherever we go, whatever we do, as native speakers of English, we are likely to be understood. Brands from English-speaking countries are global. Kentucky Fried Chicken proliferates in China: it is the country's most popular international brand with 42 branches in Beijing alone.[22] Coca-Cola is a presence and power throughout the world: the Italians have even coined a word, 'cocacolonizzare' (colonisation by Coca-Cola).[23] Even in the UK, we speak of 'McDonaldisation'. Brands, in particular those from the US, are everywhere. As Simon Anholt, the specialist in 'country branding', has said, they are globally equated with fairly much every aspect of life, from 'the definitive older male lifestyle' (Marlboro, Jack Daniel's, Ray-Ban) to food (McDonald's, Burger King, Starbucks) and travel (Hilton, Sheraton, FedEx).[24]

These brands bring both American values and English words. At the vanguard of cultural encroachment is the decision to export the same names and terms. Wherever you go, an English word is likely to get you what you want – returning to Beijing there's even – albeit controversially – a Starbucks in the Forbidden City where you can buy 'espresso beverages', 'sandwiches' and 'fruit juices'. Menus around the world are in English. As we travel on British Airways, United Airlines or Virgin jets, reaching ever more far-flung corners of the world, and as we do business with speakers of English from Bengalooru to Brasilia, we are surprised and often relieved to hear that people speak English.

However, the English language can cause resentment and the power that it represents can be felt to intrude on that represented by other languages. When the French president, Jacques Chirac, walked out of a European Council of Ministers in March 2006 he did so not through fear of the death of the French language, but the danger of its being marginalised in the world of business. His patience broke when Ernest-Antoine Seillière, the French head of the European employers' group UNICE, used English because it 'is the language of business'.[25] 'Who understands [English] words like "compliance" and "governance"?' snapped Prime Minister Koizumi of Japan in March 2006 when a questioner used English financial terms in Parliament. 'Debates shouldn't be limited to those who understand English. Debates are for everyone,' he continued.[26]

Some brands have responded to this resentment and their clients' growing awareness that it can impinge on their profit margins. HSBC markets itself as 'the world's local bank', stressing its sensitivity to local conditions, behaviour and language. In late 2006, the bank launched a website – www.yourpointofview.com – stating that 'in a world of increasing sameness, we believe it's important to value different points of view and there should be somewhere everyone can air these views and see the views of others'.[27] As the world becomes more integrated, such sensitivity is likely to be more and more important.

For the moment, however, English continues to dominate. Hollywood and English-language popular culture have taken it all over the world. *Sex and the City* sells on the black market in Beijing, and artists from Elvis Presley and The Beatles to U2 have taken English-language songs to global audiences. In the world of business, of Forbes' 2004 list of the top 2000 companies, 54 per cent have their headquarters in countries in which English is the first language, and that is discounting countries like Finland, the Netherlands and others in which English competency is very high indeed.[28] Nine out of the top ten are based in either the UK or the US (figure 3). As figure 4 shows, of the top 100, though, the percentage is even larger.

The only non-English native-speaking representative in the top ten is Toyota of Japan. China has just 25 companies in the top 2000, with the first, PetroChina, at 55. India features 27 times, but has no mention in the top 100. It still makes economic sense to speak and learn English. Even in France, 16 of 26 top firms – including AXA, Danône and Renault – have English as their working language.[29] English can also provide a usefully neutral language: when, in 1999, Rhône-Poulenc merged with Germany's Hoechst to form Aventis (number 108 on the list), it was chosen as the working language to avoid cultural tensions.[30]

The shift to commerce represents a shift in direction. Where the state relied on English to communicate its authority, brands and companies rely on it to *give* them authority. While many come from English-language-speaking countries in the first place, brands, companies and popular culture must respond to markets and, even where a market is created, it must make sense to the people with

Figure 3 The world's largest companies by country of origin

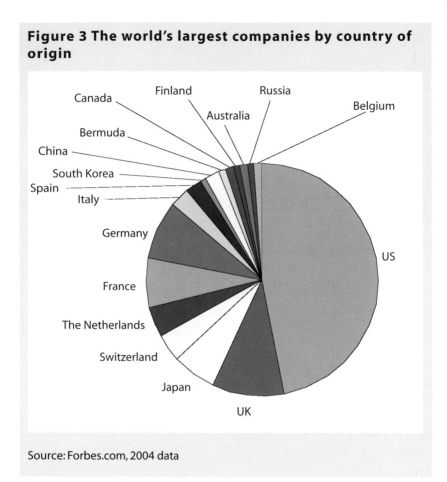

Source: Forbes.com, 2004 data

purchasing power. If English was not the global power that it was, then it could well have given way to local languages. In the age of commerce and capitalism and beyond, power has been firmly linked to individual choice.

Globalisation: opportunity for the many

There is a significant caveat to be made to the Forbes list. Many major companies outsource their business. Business process outsourcing

Figure 4 English-speaking nations dominate the list of the world's top 100 companies

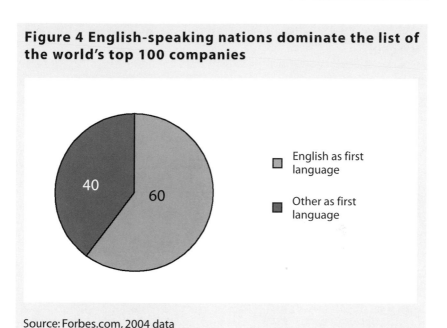

English as first language

Other as first language

Source: Forbes.com, 2004 data

(BPO) and information technology outsourcing (ITO) are major industries, especially in the financial services. Furthermore, this is shifting to practice as much as function: BPO's share of the global outsourcing market increased from 24 per cent in 2003 to 34 per cent in 2004.[31] Even one Savile Row tailor is known to measure clients in W1 and outsource the manufacture to China.[32] Call centres and service provision are outsourced to companies and workers in the developing world where skills and labour levels are high and employment costs are low. This is coming to drive the dominance of major western companies that are relying on the more economically powerful developing countries like China and India as countries in which to seek BPO providers.[33] Business trends have reinforced the strength of global English. However, they can also contribute to its diversity. This is the negotiation between master and subject to which Niall Ferguson referred. The growth of knowledge in countries like China and India and the sheer size of their populations mean that the

Anglophone dominance of the Forbes list is unlikely to remain the same for long.

Nevertheless, the economic advantages that English offers remain an advantage, and this dominance is cultural as well. This is driven by the commerce of mass media. Of 467 films released in the UK in 2005, 256 were of either UK or US origin; in terms of the revenue that they generated, a total of £844.9 million, these films accounted for £812.3 million: so, films that accounted for 55 per cent of total UK screenings generated 96 per cent of the total revenue.[34] Annually, music contributes nearly £5 billion to the UK economy, of which exports earnings account for £1.3 billion.[35] The prevalence of the English language provides the UK with direct access to the dominant cultural forms of the world today and the economic advantages that they bring.

Not forgetting the power of Caxton's initial efforts in printing, the English language has maintained its dominance in the printed word as well as the virtual. Information sources generated offline remain as dominant as ever. In 2004, 450,000 new books were published in English, 40 per cent of the worldwide total.[36] Many more are published in translation and assumptions and attitudes originally conveyed in English seep through into other languages. Harry Potter, quidditch and all, has sold 1.5 million copies in China, where selling 50,000 copies of local fiction would be regarded as very successful.[37]

This success is driven by market forces. English continues to dominate in commercial, cultural and social terms because people the world over have seized on it as offering them opportunity.

The appeal of English in Nigeria

In Nigeria, English is just one of 510 languages sitting alongside Adamawa, Edo, Efik, Fulfulde, Hausa, Idoma, Igbo, Central Kanuri and Yoruba as an official language. All of these bring tensely related histories that pre-date the arrival of English with British colonists. Both as a result but also in spite of the country's colonial past, English has maintained significance. Unofficially, about half of the population of 130 million uses a creole or pidgin English as a second language, a common medium of communication that does not so much override indigenous languages as provide a more neutral medium.

There are also other more entrepreneurial reasons for its use. A chief lecturer at Lagos State Polytechnic, Mrs Adeseye Adeyinka, puts this simply: 'The English language is the language of the mass media and of science and technology … English – and the desire to know it – is rewriting the rules of language and its role in society … transcending governments, maps and cultures.'[38]

For Mrs Adeyinka, education should give students experience of the practical aspects of their individual courses and career choices and English plays a major part in this. In professional terms, English is not simply a language for communication with the UK, US and other countries in which it is the first language, but for communicating efficiently between engineers, technicians and other professionals in specific fields. English is a means by which Nigerian interests and policy, both domestic and overseas, are best pursued.[39]

The *New York Times* journalist, Thomas Friedman, has argued that 'the world is flat'.[40] Technology and business practice, he argues, have 'flattened' the world, drawing countries, cultures and commerce together. Flat it might be, but that has only smoothed the progress of the English language and emphasised the inequalities between the English-speaking haves and the have nots. In reality, however, opportunity is not spread as liberally as the language that promises it. For one Chinese educationalist, 'people can resent others, not for speaking English, but for having access to the advantages that it offers'.[41] The question now is how English's position as the language of global opportunity will shape the power relationships with which it is associated, and in particular those that affect the UK.

Citizens: Language 2.0

Today, new technologies have influence infinitely more replicable than Caxton's press. The lesson for government and others is that, where Caxton sought premises in Westminster, the power behind changes in the English language are no longer so centralised. English is no longer spoken as a result of conquest, it is learned as a matter of choice. It is the lingua franca of a series of global communities. Where Latin and other dominant languages, including English in its past forms, represented power forced down from above, now and in the future we see a very different situation: the English language represents *access to power*.

That power is also *in aggregate*. In 1998, as Google was in its infancy, about 85 per cent of web pages were in English.[42] From this Anglophone starting point, the relationship between English and information on the internet has multiplied exponentially. When we want to research, say, 'the English language', on the internet, we type 'the English language' into a search engine. Our search generated 990 million potential sources via Google. By comparison, 'la lingua Inglese' generates a mere 4.09 million hits: that is nearly 99.6 per cent fewer than a similar process of research using the English term, 'Italian language'. This might simply be because English language mentions itself more by name than does Italian; on the other hand, even using Google.it (Google's Italian home page), 'Italy' generates 524 million hits compared with the 445 million of 'Italia'.[43]

English dominates because when we search for information, search engines find and prioritise things according to how many times overall they have been accessed and linked to. Numerically, search engines are democratic: they represent the number of times people have linked and searched for items. In terms of usage, however, the system is hegemonic: the most-used and linked-to items come out on top. The more an item is linked to, the more likely it is to be linked to the next time round and so on. In September 2006, respondents to a US survey overwhelmingly accepted 'the idea that English will be the world's lingua franca for cross-cultural communications in the next few decades'.[44] However, as global use of the internet grows, and the web truly becomes more worldwide, this is likely to change.

The internet allows different forms of English to flourish as content is added from around the world. However, these new people-driven technologies still sit within the hierarchical, authoritative and imperial structures that are reinforced by Google and other search engines. Understanding the changing power dynamics of the development of the English language is vital in creating the policy for our future.

'Now we must play internet otherwise cannot survive'

In 1999, a Singaporean published a poem on the internet. Written in 'Singlish' – the blend of English, Indic languages, Chinese dialects, Malay and Tamil – it plays on the power dynamics of the modern, globalised world. Singlish, for the author, of this poem has nationalistic symbolism. At one and the same time, the internet and globalisation are a threat to native Singaporean culture and, through Singlish, a means to reinforce it.[45]

Wah! I heard we all now got big big debate.
They said future of proper English is at stake …

Singlish is like rojak, everything throw inside anyhow mix.
Got Malay, Indian, Chinese and English, can give and take …

This kind of standard how to pass?
Wait, you sure kena last in class …

Basically Singlish got good and got bad.
Aiyah! Everything in life is all like that.

Actually Singlish got one bright side.
I am talking about our national plight …

Now we must play internet otherwise cannot survive.
Next time the only way to make money, or sure to die.

When other countries' influences all enter,
we sure kena affected left, right and centre ...

So got this kind of problem like that how?
Either sit and wait or do something now.

But actually we all got one 'culture' in Singlish.
It's like rice on the table; it is our common dish ...

Singlish is just like the garden weeds.
You pull like mad still it would not quit.

Sure got some people like and some do not like.
Singlish and English, they'll still live side by side.[46]

Although English still dominates the internet, other languages are catching up. As respondents to the US survey expected, it is likely to even out with Mandarin and other languages over the coming decades: China will have the world's largest internet population within five years. However, Paul Saffo of the Institute of the Future suggests that 'Mandarin will ... grow dramatically, but ... we will see the rise of divergent English dialects'.[47] The internet reinforces and accelerates trends in language use more widely. As people use English in their own terms, and as usage of other languages on the internet grows, the influence of the native speaker and countries like the UK and the US is eroded. The historian Eric Hobsbawm wrote that 'English has become [the] global language, even though it supplements, rather than replaces other languages'.[48] The power that English constitutes is no longer one of empire, but is becoming one of global democracy. However, just like democracy itself, the English language can suffer from a crisis of representation. The era of globalisation has been described as one in which conversations happen between people all over the world at any time. We have moved into a new phase of international relations and politics in which the constituencies are no longer national, but fragmented across borders, interests and cultures. In this system, English is a force for both coherency and accentuated difference.

3. English as a language of globalisation

The story of the English language fits into the wider context of a changing world. More people speak English in South East Asia than in Britain and North America combined and, as the world looks East for the next great economic wave, the UK's status in relation to the English language can only put it in good stead. However, it also raises an issue to which the UK must respond. As David Graddol has put it: 'English is at the centre of many globalisation mechanisms. Its future in Asia is likely to be closely associated with future patterns of globalisation.'[49]

As a result, the hierarchical picture of global English as spoken by native speakers, second-language speakers and foreign learners is no longer valid. In response, Braj Kachru has developed his model of global English to accommodate the growing importance of the *outer* circle, where English has become more proficient (figure 5).

Native speakers are no longer so distinct from those who have learned English either as a second language, or as a foreign language. In part, this reflects the development of English language provision, driven by the growing demand from overseas. However, it also reflects another change: the English spoken by people other than native speakers is reshaping the language. While the outer circle has expanded, so it has exerted a centrifugal effect on English itself, drawing its centre of gravity towards new contexts. Each year, for instance, the number of Chinese users of English grows by some 20

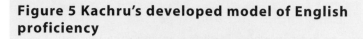

Figure 5 Kachru's developed model of English proficiency

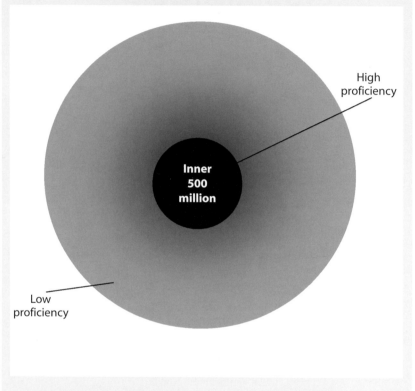

Source: From D Graddol, *English Next* (London: British Council, 2006)

million. Within the formal education sector alone, there were 176.7 million people studying English in 2005 and many others will develop rudimentary skills outside the sector.[50]

Ways of learning English around the world

The range of ways in which English is encountered around the world means that people have many opportunities to pick that language up or learn it in more formal contexts. Formally, there is a wide range of language courses provided by both native speakers and non-native speakers. Informally, words and language forms can be absorbed from popular culture and the media.

David Graddol has written that 'there is no single way of teaching English, no single way of learning it, no single motive for doing so ... no single way of assessing proficiency'.[51] It is well nigh impossible to quantify the number of people learning English, and how and where they are doing it. Nevertheless, it is possible to outline the different ways of learning English around the world. By and large, these divide between formal and informal.

Formal

There is a range of formal ways of learning English outside English-speaking countries: these divide between the curricula of national education systems and private routes. The latter can include courses run in-house by private firms training their staff in specific forms, for instance 'Business English'. Often, these will be run by private providers, who offer language courses more generally. Such organisations can provide recognised qualifications or standards. Private organisations also cooperate with international institutes, like the British Council.

Courses are also provided in developing contexts; for example, Voluntary Service Overseas (VSO) provides placements to volunteers as teachers of English on the principle that by 'providing people in developing countries with English language skills, you'll also be giving them improved access to more education and employment opportunities'.[52]

Informal

Zhang Ziyi, star of films like *Memoirs of a Geisha, Crouching Tiger: Hidden Dragon* and *Hero*, recently claimed that she began learning English by memorising lyrics from the rapper, Eminem.[53] She is just one high-profile instance of a more widespread phenomenon. The ubiquity of English-language pop culture and branding has been an important part of how English is acquired around the world.

Public organisations, like the BBC and the Voice of America, occupy the middle ground between more formal training and popular culture. As we shall see, millions in China first learned English from a popular programme broadcast by the BBC called *Follow Me*, which bridged entertainment and the provision of English language training.

As technology has developed and we have entered the information age, new popular cultures and media have come to play a significant part in the acquisition of language skills. The handheld console, Nintendo DS, has been used as a tool for learning English with specific language learning games being developed.[54] Similarly, Skype, the free voice and video chat service, hosts forums that have been used to debate why English is a common means for communication.[55]

English has come to be influenced by a wide range of different cultures and societies. As people learn English, so the norms and forms of their own tongue are likely to shape the language that they use. Words and word order are likely to change. As Kachru himself has noted, where in the UK, one might ask 'are you coming to the meeting?', in South East Asia, one might ask 'you are coming to the meeting, isn't it?'[56] Similarly, in Ghana, Nigeria and Pakistan, if you brushed your teeth, you would have 'washed your mouth'. More confusingly still, if you had been 'taken in', you would have been neither fooled nor sheltered, you would be pregnant.[57]

English is likely to be used in the expanding circle very differently from the way that it is spoken in the inner circle. The Nigerian writer Chinua Achebe put this well when he wrote:

I feel that English will be able to carry the weight of my African experience. But it will have to be a new English, still in full communion with its ancestral home but altered to suit its new African surroundings.[58]

As the distinction between native and non-native speakers of English blurs, we need to look deeper into what is going on. First, people using English around the world are not so much fitting as they are pursuing their own interests. As a result, its use is often characterised more by the desire for communicative abilities than the pursuit of standards of linguistic perfection. Second, the purpose of learning English is not so much the explicit intention of communication with native speakers, as the desire to participate in global conversations. As the Australian linguist, Joseph Lo Bianco, explains:

English is a multicultural language, used to convey, express and make possible multiple experiences in diverse societies. English is therefore a range of communication practices, accents, dialects, and a growing number of diverse national standard varieties.[59]

The export of English is demand driven, but it is not *all* market driven. As well as offering financial and commercial opportunity, it is also a means of accessing public goods, not just for native speakers, but for a global population. 'People's relationships with capitalism, modernity, democracy, aid and education', argues Sue Wright, 'are mostly mediated through English.'[60] At the same time, these concepts themselves are being renegotiated. Capitalism is giving way to globalisation, modernity to postmodernity and our concepts of democracy, aid and education are being restructured accordingly. As we go through these changes, English will be a vital link and common asset, but the advantages that we accrue as native speakers will have to be reconsidered and re-evaluated.

4. Power brings advantage

The benefits of global English

English has given the UK tremendous competitive edge. As the language of Empire it was linked to power and vestiges of that power have remained. Through institutions such as universities and the *Oxford English Dictionary*, the UK retains the idea of being the home of English. At a traditionalist level, British public schools have found a lucrative export market in China where, with an estimated 200 million people learning English, the language barrier is no longer so much of an issue. In this market, what matters most to some 150 million Chinese middle class for whom education loans can be offset against property, is a combined reverence for education and an aura of English language precision. Dulwich College was first to open a campus in Shanghai; Harrow followed soon afterwards, while a recent Beijing imitation has styled itself 'Eton'.[61]

The US domination of popular culture notwithstanding, the global media and the reputations of particular broadcasters have also reinforced the association of Britain with the English language. Alongside the US's *Voice of America*, the BBC's *World Service* has been instrumental in its spread. In 2004/05, it regularly reached an audience of more than 149 million, at least 50 per cent more than any other international radio broadcaster.[62] Individual programmes also have an impact. In China, one educationalist recalls that the BBC programme *Follow Me* influenced thousands in the early 1980s.[63] It was a learning programme hosted by Katherine Flower, a UK language teacher, aired at 6.30pm on China Central Television (CCTV). In the aftermath of the Cultural Revolution, Katherine Flower represented a lone voice from the West. According to the BBC, 'entire villages would gather around their one and only black and white television set' and China 'fell in love with the lead actor Francis Matthews, the "perfect English gentleman"'. At its peak, over 100 million people watched *Follow Me*, double the population of the UK itself.[64] Its success has continued: the production company behind the programme, which has recently been relaunched in China, now sells over 20 million books a year, 95 per cent of these in English.[65]

English also brings advantage for more contemporary reasons. It provides definite benefits to the UK overall, and it matters to individuals because in a widening variety of contexts, speaking it provides access to greater opportunity. These two areas are very much related, but they also divide into the effects felt by society as a whole, and the effects sought and pursued by individuals. In policy-making terms, this is very important: while English brings general, social and national advantage, it is also approached from very individual standpoints and provides a very individual way of experiencing the world. Policy must take both of these into account.

Overall benefits to the UK
Economic
Alone, the English language teaching sector earns nearly £1.3 billion pounds in direct revenue for the UK each year.[66] More generally, a report to the French government estimates the UK gains at least €10 billion per annum from the dominance of the English language. The report's author, François Grin, calculates that, taking into account the multiplying effects that the 'privileged position' of the English language affords, including investment from other English-speaking countries, this sum is in reality €17–18 billion.[67] All told, these sums amount to about £14.5 billion, which Grin predicts can only be increased by the precedence given to English-language competence in the education of future political leaders in non-native speaking countries.

The attraction of English-language business books

Chen Xiaohui manages the Beijing Cheers Book Company. Each year, the company publishes over 50 books on economics and management. About 80 per cent of this is driven through the copyright trade of translations from US, UK and European texts, many of which are in English. 'In the area of economic management books', Chen explained to the English-language newspaper, *China Daily*, 'foreign books have far more advantages over local ones, since those countries have had a longer time to operate as free market economies, and have accumulated much more real-hand experience than China.'[68]

China and other countries look to the US, the UK and other Anglophone countries as authorities, but as authorities from which they can learn to operate in equal, globalised markets. At the moment this drives Western economic success, but might also undermine it. Western governments need to be aware that as exporting language attracts income, so the translation of that language and learning can take it away. This is not an argument for denying access to translations. It is a call to government and others that reliance on the English language in commerce and elsewhere is living on borrowed time.

The Beijing Cheers Book Company and countless similar examples give UK policy-makers and others an important lesson. The English language does lend the UK economic competitiveness, and there is certainly little incentive to the UK government or private interests in this country to prevent it. However, the issue is in whether that competitiveness will remain and the legitimacy and implications of the approaches that the UK adopts in seeking to ensure that it does.

Social mobility

Lingua franca status means that it is easier for native English speakers to travel and communicate overseas. Equally, with global travel and tourists visiting new countries and markets the incentive for others to learn English is great. One high-profile example is 'Beijing speaks English', the campaign mentioned earlier to develop skills in English prior to 2008. Officially, the focus is infrastructure: taxi drivers will have to develop relevant English skills and 80 per cent of police officers under 40 will have to attain basic levels of communicative proficiency. However, it is also likely to extend to individuals seeking to make the most of the visit of multiple nationalities for whom English is the lingua franca. 'Beijing speaks English' illustrates a growing trend of accommodation by speakers of other languages to the market forces that English represents. Economically, this offers the UK and other native speakers opportunities for trade and investment.

There are also other benefits to be gained. Much attention is paid to the importance of diaspora groups in the UK, especially in terms of social cohesion, but little is paid to the increasing numbers of UK citizens living and working abroad. In a survey conducted by the Institute for Public Policy Research for the BBC in August 2006, nearly 13 per cent of UK citizens said they would consider emigration in the near future.[69] Similarly, around 800,000 British households now own a second home abroad, a rise of 45 per cent since June 2004.[70]

We must seek to re-engage with our diaspora communities. As other countries become more proficient in English, so they will grow in popularity as destinations for emigration and tourism. Some communities are already significant economic and social forces. The British Chamber of Commerce in Thailand, for instance, was founded in 1946 with 17 members and has grown to become the country's largest non-Asian foreign chamber with a membership of over 620 companies, seeing a 77 per cent rise in the last nine years.[71]

We need to encourage relationships between expats and English language learners. Expats are likely to be the first point of contact between foreign publics and the UK; for learners of English who have never been to these shores, they are also likely to be the only point of contact. Rather than seeing the skills of speakers of other languages as making it easier for people to do business and get around, it is also important that we recognise that it makes it easier for them to find out about the UK. Our diaspora could well prove to be one of our greatest assets in public diplomacy, helping bolster the image of the UK overseas.

Cultural experience

Increased social mobility also brings greater exposure to different cultures. In 2005, the number of tourists worldwide amounted to 800 million people, up 5.5 per cent from 2004, which in itself represented a rise of 10 per cent from 2003.[72] We are travelling more than ever. According to Office of National Statistics figures, we are also travelling to more diverse destinations, in particular Anglophone countries like Australia, New Zealand and South Africa.[73] Furthermore, where visits to France have decreased in the past five years, trips to China, India and African countries in which English competency is high have increased. On our travels, we are encountering a more diverse range of people than ever before. While cultures and societies can best be accessed in their native languages, the fact that many are communicating in the English language opens a far wider range of experience to us. In the world's major tourist sites, guidebooks, notices, labels and audioguides are usually available in English, and tourist boards, like Dublin's, now offer podcasts in English to download prior to your visit.[74] Visitors to the Forbidden City in Beijing can learn about emperors like Qianlong and Xuantong via an audioguide narrated by Sir Roger Moore. Elsewhere in China, Western visitors to the town of Yangshuo might be surprised to meet Mama Moon and her colleagues, farmers offering tours in English.[75] From *Fodor* to *Frommers* and *Lonely Planet*, and now the iPod, English has been key to tourism. It is not only through travel that we gain greater exposure to different cultures and contexts. New technologies bring these experiences directly into our homes: as the internet has grown and the platforms for cultural exchange and the transmission of cultural goods has developed, a new cultural environment has emerged in which the English language dominates.

This hegemony also extends to the media and current affairs. News channels reveal English's dominance as a means of accessing current affairs. BBC World is watched more than any of its other channels. Furthermore, al-Jazeera is not alone in launching an English news channel from a non-native speaking country. More niche channels are set to join the Anglophone news stream: in Germany there is 'Deutsche Welle', in Russia 'Russia Today' and Iran has recently announced a 24-hour news channel called 'Press'. Perhaps most surprisingly of all given Francophone sensitivity, the French government has recently collaborated with leading network, TF1 to launch 'France 24', a French news provider, broadcasting in English.[76]

English is the language of a global culture. Even a dubbed film promotes the ideologies and attitudes of its makers.[77] As English is spread, the advantages that native speakers have in this cultural world are clear. Lord Carter of Coles, in his 2005 *Public Diplomacy Review*, noted of the British Council that 'English language teaching and exams, as well as attracting students to study in the UK were also undertaken to draw more people into a relationship with the UK, and help expose them to information and activities about the UK.'[78]

English provides a medium by which different cultures can communicate their values, outlooks and beliefs. Writers like Salman Rushdie use it to explore identity and faith. As he sees it: 'The children of independent India seem not to think of English as being irredeemably tainted by its colonial provenance. They use it as an Indian language, as one of the tools they have to hand.'[79] As novelists and others use English in this way, the cultures to which it gives us access multiply. Some Indian authors, like Nirad Chaudhuri, switch between English and other languages for different audiences.[80] In the UK, the comedian Meera Syal has used 'Hinglish' in a way that reflects the cultural mix of the UK's streets, playgrounds and workplaces[81] and, in February 2007, her writing was put on the National Curriculum.[82]

Science, technology and innovation

Science and technology and the terms that they generate have enriched the English language. As Anglophone countries led the way in innovation, so English came to represent it. Nearly half of the scientists working between 1750 and 1900 worked in English and several more were collaborating with English-speaking scholars.[83] In the seventeenth century, mathematics and anatomy generated a new lexicon and, from the beginning of the nineteenth century, further discoveries and disciplines demanded new designations. 'Chlorophyll' was coined in 1819, 'caffeine' in 1830, and 'palaeontology' in 1838.[84] This linguistic influx has continued. As the US and Silicon Valley have led the field in IT, words like 'software', the 'internet' and IT itself have become common parlance across the world. Brand names like Apple, Microsoft, Windows and Intel have similarly linked IT and technological innovation firmly to English.

The dominance of English words also extends to the domain itself. When asked to speak on English as the language of science, one Catalan scientist was nonplussed:

I had never thought it possible that the language used in such exchanges would be a possible matter for debate.[85]

In October 2006, the publisher Blackwell announced that two of its English-language journals had won an award for being among the top five Chinese science and technology journals.[86] English speakers can access, read and respond to literature and papers more easily than can, say, a scientist who speaks only Korean or Mandarin.

English is by far and away the most-used language in science (see figure 6). Chinese is increasing, but is a force for the future. The rapid decline of publication in Russian, coincident with the fall of the USSR, reflects the close association of power and language. In this light, the erosion of German and French will do little to allay Jacques Chirac's fears for the wider use of the French language. It is not that French and German publication is unimportant: it is more that scientists consider that using English reaches wider audiences. In global terms, this is an essential driver of science and innovation, which depend on the networks of individuals and ideas that English supports.

Figure 6 Language used in *Chemical Abstracts* (1961–2005)

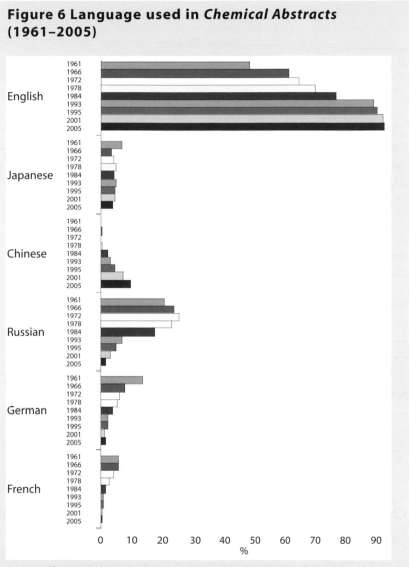

Source: *Chemical Abstracts, Statistical Summary 1907–2005* (Columbus, Ohio: American Chemical Society, 2006)

However, neither local specialisms nor material written in other languages can be sidelined by wider readerships. It is essential that knowledge is shared and promoted, and ways should be found to draw these in. The SARS epidemic in China showed all too clearly that shared knowledge is vital. When the virus struck in Spring 2003, Beijing sought to conceal knowledge of its spread. However, in a democratic twist of power, millions of Chinese used mobile phones and the internet to access foreign news reports and information to get a clearer picture of what was going on.[87] On the one hand, we need to maintain an ecology of local knowledge; on the other, we need to find ways to draw it together. As the political scientist Jean Laponce has argued, at the moment English is the surest way of doing this. His argument that 'the expenditure should be on the side of English as a second language in order that French scientists and students have universal access to the findings published in the language of chemistry' could well apply in global terms as well.[88]

Individual interest

While maintaining the advantages that English offers, we need also to respond to the more citizen and individually driven momentum that propels the way that it is used around the world today.

Community cohesion

The UK's leaders have had the most to say about the English language in relation to citizenship. In December 2006, Prime Minister Tony Blair announced that:

> It is a matter both of cohesion and of justice that we should set the use of English as a condition of citizenship. In addition, for those who wish to take up residence permanently in the UK, we will include a requirement to pass an English test before such permanent residency is granted.[89]

His words echoed those of Chancellor Gordon Brown a few months before:

It is right that people who come to and are in this country to stay learn English; have some sense of what it means to be British, of our history and our culture; and through citizenship tests and citizenship ceremonies take British citizenship seriously.[90]

In the UK, there are 1.9 million learners of English for Speakers of Other Languages (ESOL). That number is likely to grow. The demand for ESOL has tripled since 2001 – enrolment among Polish nationals alone increased from 151 in 2000/01 to 21,313 in 2004/05.[91] However, where the government looks to English in terms of Britishness, speaking English also offers learners the chance to communicate their own values. We need to access and build from the cultural experience and knowledge that they bring and the experiences of the UK that they have. For Bill Rammell, Minister for Further Education and Lifelong Learning, we need to focus 'on developing the basic skills to improve social mobility and cohesion, with ESOL provision obviously playing a particularly important part'.[92]

He was commenting on a report from the National Institute for Adult Continuation in Education (NIACE) *More than a Language,* which concluded that 'ESOL provision is critically important to the UK. It is essential to help secure social inclusion and build stable and successful communities, and it underpins current policy on citizenship and settlement.'[93] However, too often this is seen from an instrumentalist point of view, determined less by what learners actually need, and more by the value that they can add.

The way in which this can be overcome is by combining wider social needs with individual interests. 'Personalisation through participation', writes Charles Leadbeater, 'makes the connection between the individual and the collective by allowing users a more direct, informed and creative say in rewriting the script by which the service they use is designed, planned, delivered and evaluated.'[94] ESOL provision to newcomers to the UK must take this principle on board.

An individual's immediate concerns are likely to be well-being and employment – immigrants who speak English to a reasonable proficiency are 20 per cent more likely to find work and earn on average 18–20 per cent more than those who do not.[95] However, beyond this, feelings of security and happiness come through cross-cultural communication. This means not just integration and assimilation, but real *two-way* communication of values and ideals, complemented by support focused on learners' needs.

> ### The needs of learners in the UK
> Speaking at the launch of *More than a Language*, Hortance Mbelu, a migrant to the UK, said:
>
> *I came to the UK in 2001.... The beginning is the most difficult time because you have a lot of problems.... You are a stranger in a new country. You don't even know one word, but you have to live there and, without English, you can do nothing. I don't want to live on benefits. I want to finish my course and get a good job. The best thing is when you can communicate with people, when you can hear the radio and follow the TV, read newspapers. You feel free.[96]*

It is important to engage learners like Hortance on their own terms. Language liberates, allowing the expression of viewpoints and opinion. The Brazilian pedagogical theorist Paolo Freire wrote that 'the more the oppressors control the oppressed, the more they change them into apparently inanimate "things".[97] Freire's terminology is harsh, but it contains valuable lessons for ESOL provision. Integration does not necessarily mean assimilation. Learners must be given the skills both to lead a full and fair life in the UK and by which they can bring their own experiences to the communities that they develop and enter, enriching UK society.

Opportunity and foreign travel

While increased mobility and travel benefit society as a whole, they are driven by personal and individual interest. English provides individuals and companies with access to different destinations and markets. On one level, this is practical – English-language road signs make major cities like Beijing and Tokyo much more accessible and navigable to English-speaking visitors. On another, for the economic reasons we have seen, the English language creates opportunities the world over.

Widespread interest in English also means that there is demand for native English speakers to teach it overseas. Teaching English as a Foreign Language (TEFL) and Teaching English as a Second Language (TESOL) are popular choices for young graduates today. This gives young people easy access to career opportunities, travel and life experiences that are less available to speakers of other languages.

5. The modern reality of global English

In this global world not knowing English can be a disadvantage,
but knowing only English can also be a disadvantage.

Joseph Lo Bianco[98]

The situation in the largest English-speaking country in the world

The ages of 'commerce and capitalism' and the 'Language 2.0' are characterised by Wall St and Google, respectively. As a result, one might expect the American heirs of William Penn, John Adams and their peers to be reaping the benefits that the English language provides. However, in the land that has given us words from racoon to hamburger and that has done most to spread English around the world, all does not appear so rosy.

The Library of Congress is the oldest federal cultural institution in the US, sharing its origins with Washington itself. Outside the Library, when it rains, or when the floor is washed, temporary signs on the sidewalk advise both 'caution, wet floor' and '*cuidado, piso mojado*' (figure 7). For all the classicised architecture of Washington, the key to power in the US today is in appealing to multicultural and multilingual concerns. For the Library's resources to be available and useful to the Congress and the American people, they need also to be in Spanish.

The sign in figure 7 shows linguistic diversity, but it doesn't quite

Figure 7 Warning sign outside the Library of Congress, Washington DC

Source: Photograph Samuel Jones

tell the full story. In late 2006, the Royal Academy of Arts in London put on an exhibition of contemporary art from the US. It included work that was challenging, complaining and on occasion cathartic. It was an exhibition that heralded malaise and ill-feeling. Looking at it, one got a feeling of deflation, like that of a riotous party, still raging, but with the clock ticking and taxis arriving. In one image, a girl stares coolly and seductively from a glossy photo, a lit match hanging casually from her lips, burning brightly but slowly towards her flesh. In another, the artist Matthew Day Jackson presents a seemingly haphazard mix of photographs, prints and other media. It tells a political story imbued with language and linguistic politics today. Jackson's *Dance of Destruction* parodies the current state of the US. We see an eighteenth-century folk landscape, familiar from so many cosy American histories but, erupting from the foreground is another familiar image: the Tower of Babel. Babel is a familiar myth, but what is it doing here? In an image critiquing the US's contradictions, the problem of language pokes rudely through an otherwise homely scene. Why, in the largest native English-speaking country in the world, is language presented as such a disruptive and confusing force?

Despite the apparent dominance of English in the US, there are thousands of stories that demonstrate multilingualism. Banks, such as Chase and Bank of America, have offered financial services in both English and Spanish since the 1980s.[99] According to one American professor, 'Spanglish represents the most important contemporary linguistic phenomenon in the United States'.[100] He refers to a sign in Miami Dade County Jail that offers visitors three versions of a much-needed protocol:

Visitors to this facility must be escorted by an officer at all times [English]

Los visitantes de esta facilidad deben ser todo el tiempo escortados por un official [Spanglish]

Los visitants de esta instalación deben estar todo el tiempo acompañados por un guardia [Spanish]

In fact, according to *Ethnologue*, the database of languages, the overall number of living languages in the US is 162.[101] Annandale, a small suburb of Washington DC is known as Koreatown: as with areas of other cities that have acquired a similar epithet, signs on the high street are subtitled in English.[102] Such multilingualism has led to anxiety and tension. Congress has passed provisions for language minorities to ensure adequate representation in the electoral process. On 18 May 2006, the Senate voted to designate English as the national language. Note, 'national' and not 'official': language choice is being used to assert identity as much as it is to ensure administrative efficiency. At the same time, a controversial version of 'The Star-Spangled Banner' appeared: the words famous from countless schoolrooms, Olympic ceremonies and baseball games crashed out in Spanish.[103] It was called 'Nuestro Himno', 'Our Hymn'. 'Would the French accept people singing the 'La Marseillaise' in English as a sign of French patriotism? Of course not,' responded Mark Krikorian, head of the Washington-based Center for Immigration Studies.[104] Even President George W Bush has been drawn into the debate, offering a reminder that 'one of the important things here is, when we debate this issue, that we not lose our national soul'.[105] In the run-up to the mid-term elections in November 2006, debate continued about multilingual ballot papers. Some feared that those against the idea had bound more exclusive motives ('if you can't speak English, should you vote?') into their arguments and proposed a bill to prevent it; Senator Harry Reid of Nevada, the Democrat leader in the Senate, condemned the bill as being racist.

Debates in the US about language stem from the close connection between language and power: whose voice and experiences does the English language permit and reflect? Although it is the largest native English-speaking country in the world, what is happening in the US mirrors what is happening elsewhere. The dominance of English can cause tension. At the same time, it is becoming increasingly difficult for native English-speaking countries to exist with conventional definitions of the language. If this is the situation in the largest native English-speaking nation in the world, then what is it like in the UK, the historical home of the English language?

English language and the UK

The situation in the UK is similarly complex. In Wales, road signs are in Welsh as well as English, and in Birmingham, they are in Urdu. The UK's multilingualism is one of its greatest social and cultural assets. However, it can also be one of its weaknesses and, too often, we pay little attention to the cultural wealth that it offers.

Social mobility and increased immigration mean that there is a rich cultural mix in which languages play a major part. Between them, London's schoolchildren speak 300 different languages, double the number in the US: 76 are spoken in the borough of Tower Hamlets alone. This diversity runs throughout the UK. In the north west of England, schoolchildren speak a combined total of 139 languages. Multilingualism means diversity; however, it also brings questions of integration and immersion. The hows and whys of language provision to new learners raise issues of legitimacy and cultural equality. While we need to provide newcomers to the UK with language skills that help them integrate into the structures of society, there is also a responsibility to provide them with the skills by which they can use the English language to talk about their different cultural experiences and identities.

Languages enable people to bond as communities, but they can also be used as statements and messages of difference. Government within the UK has been devolved and we now have separate Scottish and Welsh Assemblies. This independence is reflected in language. Once in decline, Welsh has seen a resurgence: conscious of the power of the internet in shaping language use, the Welsh Language Board is campaigning for companies and others to offer bilingual options, rather than simply English services.[106] Similarly, alongside languages that range from Gaelic to Bengali and Italian, the Scottish Parliament has a section in 'Scots' (see figure 8).

In global terms, resistance to English has long and established links to nationalism and the rejection of Western values or influence. In 1908, a century before Beijing made its bid to 'Speak English', Mahatma Gandhi wrote that 'to give millions a knowledge of English is to enslave them'.[107]

Foreign-language learning in the UK

Gandhi was speaking of British hegemony in India. However, a similar sentiment might be expressed of perceptions in the UK of English's global currency. Much is made of the diversity of linguistic life in the UK but, still, languages do not figure highly in the nation's considerations. There is a real need to raise awareness of just how important languages, including English in its different forms, will be to our future.[108]

Figure 8 The Scots language on the Scottish Parliament website

Source: www.scottish.parliament.uk/vli/language/scots/index.htm

In December 2006, 50 leading UK academics called jointly for the government to reverse its recent decision to allow pupils to drop languages at 14: one called the decision 'benighted' and another called it 'absolutely crazy'.[109] For years, news reports and articles have argued the need to encourage more of our pupils to learn foreign languages. Agnès Poirier, a French journalist, drew attention to our disappearing language skills. She called it 'Britain's dirty little secret'.[110] In 2002, the ambassadors of France, Germany, Italy and Spain asked the government to address the issue of language learning in state schools.[111] Late in 2006, the German ambassador reiterated this plea, saying that 'the greatest task probably lies in raising awareness among the British public. In the home country of English, the world language, the task of persuasion is especially difficult.'[112]

Government is going some way to address this. In February 2007, it announced plans to offer 11–14-year-olds in England languages like Mandarin. Furthermore, the Secretary of State for Education, Alan Johnson, said recently that:

> *There is a problem in this country: people who speak three languages are called trilingual, people who speak two languages are called bilingual, and those who speak one language are called English.*[113]

Of all our European counterparts, we have the highest number of citizens who speak no language except their mother tongue.[114] Between 2005 and 2006, the number of candidates taking GCSE French fell by 13.2 per cent, while the number taking German fell by 14.2 per cent. Between 1999 and 2002, 'UK students taking languages at English universities fell by 15 per cent . . . undergraduate numbers in strategically important languages . . . like Arabic, Chinese and Japanese, have also fallen by 12 per cent, 16 per cent and 27 per cent, respectively.'[115]

While our language skills decline, government seems to be looking the other way: foreign language learning for post-14-year-olds has recently been made voluntary. Owning up to this policy, the former Secretary of State for Education, Estelle Morris, wrote recently that 'foreign languages are far more important than we've ever recognised and every child should study them. I bemoan our national lethargy and poor performance as linguists.' She argues that 'the idea that we can turn this around by forcing reluctant 14–16-year-olds to carry on with French, or any other language, seems a bit unlikely'.[116]

The answer to our linguistic deficiency lies in addressing young people's linguistic skills in the long term, especially given that children pick up language skills more readily than do adults.[117] David Graddol's pamphlet, *English Next*, has paved the way for thinking about the implications of global English on the interests of countries in which English is the native tongue.[118] In introducing the pamphlet, Lord Kinnock wrote that 'monoglot English graduates face a bleak economic future as qualified multilingual youngsters from other countries are proving to have competitive advantage over their British counterparts in global companies and organisations'.[119] From his perspective as a former European Commissioner, Lord Kinnock is only too aware of the inadequacy of linguistic competence in the UK.

Evidence abounds that access to markets trading in English will increasingly be scant consolation for the costs of monolingualism. In 2004, three surveys put this beyond doubt. The first, for the British Chambers of Commerce, found that 80 per cent of export managers cannot competently conduct dealings in even one foreign language.[120] Another found that the proportion of UK executives capable of negotiating in more than one language was half that of the rest of the EU, and well below the global average.[121] Finally, a Federation of Small Businesses membership survey revealed foreign languages as one of three key skills areas in which businesses felt the greatest dissatisfaction.[122]

In focusing on our linguistic skills, we should not blinker ourselves to another point. While our language skills leave much to be desired, one cliché – the impeccable English of the foreigner – rings as uncomfortably true as another: the Englishman abroad shouting slowly from a menu in English. The two are very closely related. As English has become a basic skill around the world the natural advantage of the native speaker has been whittled away. When Indian companies can train native English speakers in Belfast as call-centre operatives, English no longer privileges the native speaker in quite such clear terms.[123]

Interviewing people in China, we spoke to them in English and not Mandarin because we were the ones who could not use Mandarin. Yes, the reasons for speaking English in that context might be derived from British hegemony in the past and the prevalence of English as a business tongue, but the power relationship has changed. It is more telling of the future that the Chinese people of all ages to whom we spoke can choose to speak English with us and Chinese with their family, friends and colleagues. There is no class status, merely a situation in which the native speaker is at a disadvantage.

In the past, it stood to reason that learners of English would seek teaching from a native-speaking provider. Today, the choice is less clear cut. The combination of travel and accommodation costs and relatively high prices for courses in the UK or US means that people choose providers closer to home. As one UK provider has commented: 'There is a tendency for students to remain in their own countries because many new students come from less affluent groups.'[124] Alongside such economic rationales, many learners also have pragmatic reasons for seeking English from non-native-speaking providers. In China, some universities are using Belgian companies to develop lessons for English language curricula. The thinking is that Belgians, like the Chinese, are second-language speakers and so understand the needs of learning languages as adults and communicating between non-native speakers.[125] More and more, people see the need to learn the language not because they want to communicate more easily with native speakers, but because they want to partake in a global conversation. A recent report for the British Council suggested that pragmatic reasons for learning English – in international, business or social contexts – lay far less emphasis on British culture and values than might models of learning in the past.[126]

How is the government to respond? The English language is a vital part of our economy, identity and power, but with directive action comes the spectres of linguistic imperialism and language death. As the Foundation for Endangered Languages puts it: 'There is agreement among linguists that . . . within perhaps two generations, most languages in the world will die out.'[127] At least 50 per cent of the world's 6000 languages are likely to die within a century. With English as the world's language, we need to identify how and where language policy is appropriate and in what contexts promoting it is legitimate.

Some fear that the dominance of English will have severe consequences for the globe's linguistic diversity. The linguist Robert Phillipson worries that 'with the commercial world setting the pace, and with the encroachment of English into countless spheres of public and private life, it is arguable that all European languages other than English may be on the fast track towards second-class status'.[128] However, as David Crystal argues, 'the emergence of any one language as global has only a limited causal relationship to this unhappy state of affairs'.[129]

Global linguistic diversity is essential. Languages interrelate and feed each other: for example, it is from the French 'gauffre' that we derive the name for 'gopher' in reference to its waffle-like pelt. For the novelist Anthony Burgess 'language flowers in ways that English will never understand'. He cites the Australian Aboriginal language, Dyirbal, by way of demonstration. In Dyirbal, the belief that women turn into birds after death is reflected in its grammatical structure: a feminine class marker is always followed by a nominal, denoting a bird.[130] Unfortunately, according to *Ethnologue*, only 40–50 speakers of Dyirbal remain.[131]

We need to protect and preserve languages, and Phillipson and others rightly cite the United Nations *Declaration on the Rights of Persons Belonging to National or Ethnic, Religious and Linguistic Minorities* (1992).[132] Speakers of the world's ten most spoken languages account for about half of its population, leaving a 'long tail' of nearly 6500 languages rich in global heritage and culture: at least 10 per cent of these have 100 or fewer speakers. The problem also extends to major languages, including French, German and Italian. They will not die out – French has 175 million speakers and the second-largest francophone city in the world is Kinshasa – but the fear, as we have seen, is that they might be marginalised by English in contexts like business and politics. Native speakers of English need to be much more aware of the antagonism this can cause.

Currently, the UK's approach to the English language can appear damagingly outmoded and inconsiderate of these concerns. Phillipson's definition of English linguistic imperialism as 'referring to the explicit and implicit values, beliefs, purposes, and activities which characterise the ELT profession and which contribute to the maintenance of English as a dominant language'[133] sticks in the mind.

The steamroller effect of English has come to be resented by native speakers of other languages. For example, the Académie Française is explicit in its mission:

> *The influence of the French language is threatened by the expansion of the English – to be more precise the American – language, which has taken hold of spirits, writing and the modern communications world.*
>
> *The growth of English is often spurred on by technical revolution, accelerated scientific innovation and the remarkable 'rapprochement' that the media and other communicative forms allow, all factors that have pushed aside traditional vocabulary and have led to the rapid adoption of new words.*[134]

Part of the backlash against global English is the reassertion of local languages on the grounds of identity. In India, the European names for cities like Bombay, Calcutta and Madras have been dropped in favour of the previous regional names, Mumbai, Kolkata and Chennai, respectively. In November 2006, Bangalore formally reverted to Bengalooru, its name in the local language, Kannada. Recently, the education minister of Bengalooru threatened to close 2000 private schools in the state of Karnataka that teach primarily in English. In so doing, the region has mirrored West Bengal's 'No English, only Bengali' policy.[135]

Such rejection of English is unlikely to undermine its global status. However, it does reveal why the UK should be careful to manage its relationship with its native language. While it brings us opportunity, it can also create resentment and, in an age in which power is shifting to these new contexts of usage, the consequences will be dramatic.

The English language in developing contexts

On its website, the UK Department for International Development lists the following operational values:

o   ambition and determination to eliminate poverty

O   diversity and the need to balance work and private life
O   ability to work effectively with others
O   desire to listen, learn and be creative
O   professionalism and knowledge.[136]

Respectively, English has a role to play in all of these areas:

O   Aid is provided through networks and communication
      dependent on English.
O   International organisations and even countries, like
      Nigeria, use English as a common and neutral medium
      amid cultural diversity although, increasingly, it is to the
      advantage of the English learner over the native speaker
      that he or she can speak a native tongue as well.
O   English provides a common means of communication.
O   As a global language, English is also an entrepôt of
      cultures.
O   English provides global access to professions and
      knowledge.

As well as contributing to governmental objectives, this developmental role fits with the global role of the BBC. The BBC has become
much more than simply a vehicle for communicating British interest.
It has also been welcomed around the world as providing news and
information and, as the example of *Follow Me* demonstrates, access to
the English language. As it positions itself in the UK as a body that
delivers public value, through its international position, and through
the English language, it also delivers public value on a global stage.

   The idea of British governmental bodies and the BBC as delivering
global public value is important and points to a new relationship
between English and the UK. Where, in the days of Empire, English
represented the voice of authority, now it represents many more
voices that belong to many different people all over the world. In
1997, the US author Eric Raymond wrote an essay on developments
in software engineering called *The Cathedral and the Bazaar*.[137] The

cathedral describes the prescriptive, dogmatic provision of proprietary software, and is contrasted with the multivocal bazaar of open-source programming. In its shift from the imperial to the globalised phase, English has gone through similar changes. We can no longer see it in the same terms as did missionaries and colonists and it is certainly not seen that way by people using English today. Instead, global English is a means for all to pursue their own interests.

> ### A twenty-first century adaptation of the Macaulay minute
>
> In 1834, the chairman of the Governor-General's Committee on Public Instruction, Lord Macaulay, wrote a minute to the British Governor of India, Lord Bentinck. He proposed that education in India should be in English. This set the tone for the next 150 years, linking English to privilege and status.
>
> On the 206th anniversary of Lord Macaulay's birth, Dalit activists proclaimed their worship of a new goddess – the English language.[138] The Dalits are the 'untouchables' of India – a 250-million-strong group dealing with the legacy of a caste system still relevant in practice if not policy. The new deity is far more than a publicity stunt. According to The Dalit Freedom Network: 'The greatest opportunities in Indian society and around the world are offered to those … that have been educated in English, as well as in their own local dialect.'[139]
>
> The Dalits' celebration demonstrates the power politics associated with English. It shows how it is seen as being vital to social and economic welfare. Originally introduced to the middle classes of Indian society, English was the language of the administrative elites and was central in maintaining colonial presence. The Dalits were using English to demand equal opportunity. In their hands, it became a means of exposing social injustices that prevent social equality of opportunity and welfare.

At the same time as people use it in their own terms the world over, it is undeniable that the prevalence of English in the global economic system is of massive benefit to the US and the UK. It is nevertheless misleading to draw too simple a parallel between English speaking and the interests of native speakers. There is a need to balance the concern of others and tension caused by memories of colonial power. Learning English has become a global choice, and one which subsequently brings huge benefits. But that choice is also, in part, a legacy of the power relations of Empire. Even in developmental contexts, the use of the English language carries with it Anglo-American assumptions of what development means and should look like. As a result, it is not surprising that examples of English being resented can be found almost as frequently as examples of its being adopted. From Gandhi to the revival of Welsh and Scots, this has been associated with nationalistic beliefs that the UK would do well to avoid crossing. In shaping policy, we need to understand the tensions between the old models of power that saw the imposition of English and the emerging dynamics created by flows of capital and people, and the complex factors that constitute people's choices.

If English is a global asset, then Robert Phillipson's reminder that 'we have to investigate . . . the manifestly false promises to have-nots about the acquisition of (some) competence in English leading them towards economic prosperity' has great value.[140] While direct and immediate concerns – such as poverty and hunger – take precedence, provision of English where it is needed could contribute to development objectives. We need to consider how, in providing English language skills, learners can also be given the opportunity to use them. English is not a route to immediate prosperity, but it is a route to developing skills bases and long-term opportunities for people in developing contexts.

6. Fiddling while Rome burns

As a living language, will there arrive a point when we will no longer be able to understand English as spoken by other nations and cultures?
Lord Watson, chairman of Corporate Television Networks and Burson-Marsteller, Europe[141]

In September 2006, an Indian journalist filed a report from Kolkata for the *Asian Times*. It began with 'an alert for all monolingual speakers of native English: if you thought your ability to speak English would continue to give you a leg-up in the world . . . you are in for trouble'.[142] As more and more people speak English, economic benefits will slip; however, as we shall see, there are also more social problems that might arise.

Initially, it is in economic and commercial terms that the warning in the *Asian Times* rings clearest. Simon Anholt has written that 'even having an English-language slogan no longer necessarily means you come from an English-speaking country: it just means you're an international brand'.[143] From government to businesses and individuals, the UK relies too readily on monolingualism in what is rapidly becoming a world of competitive multilingualism.

The same applies to businesses and organisations. The Asian trade group ASEAN – the Association of South East Asian Nations – has English as the working language, but its employees are multilingual.

In the UK in 2005, the National Centre for Languages (CILT) researched language competence in major companies across Europe and the US. In France and Germany, over 75 per cent of multinationals included language skills in their policies for recruitment; only 30 per cent of their UK counterparts did the same, even though 72 per cent of UK trade is with countries that do not have English as their first language. This in a sample in which 'some 75–80 per cent of UK multinationals expressed a desire to work . . . only in English'.[144]

Even if they do work 'only in English', what kind of English will it be? We cannot continue to rely on it in the way that we have. We must respond to the ways in which English is developing. There are about 900,000 words in English. This vast lexicon has seen a boost of late. Words from hyphenated languages like Chinese-English (Chinglish) and, as we have seen, Hindi-English (Hinglish) and Singlish have added rich new vocabulary. However, this is a world away from the everyday experience of individual speakers of English. David Crystal estimates that you or I will use only about 40,000 words and know probably another 20,000.[145] That is about a twentieth of the vocabulary available to us. We use and encounter words in familiar contexts, between friends and family or in the workplace. However, there are English speakers doing exactly the same thing, from a different education base, on the other side of the world. Now, with changes in the way we communicate and increased social mobility, it is more likely than ever that we will come across people using a different set of words in different contexts.

Linguistically, this is unlikely to pose serious problems in the near or even foreseeable future; what will be more problematic is the fragmentation of communities that it could represent. Eric Hobsbawm and others have demonstrated the importance of languages in shaping a community. George Bernard Shaw's oft-quoted distinction between England and the US as being 'divided by a common language' draws on this very concept. English is fast becoming a language family, rather than a language. This could create starker boundaries between different linguistic communities. Already – as

Meera Syal and the *Goodness, Gracious Me* team have played on – distinct and recognisable forms of English have come to represent cultural groups. Often, language use is dependent on identity and individual purpose, even in formal settings. Geographically, individual regions will appropriate standard versions of a language as a mark of distinctiveness: as for the Singlish poet mentioned earlier and the Scottish Parliament, distinction can also be a point of defiance.

We have always had different forms of English, from regional accents within the UK to American, Australian and South African English. Now these forms could come to mirror and ultimately reinforce sociocultural divides on a much more global scale. Names like Hinglish and Chinglish both explain their hybrid origins and imply that they are corruptions of English. We must find ways to manage this development not by cramping the enrichment of the lexis and structures of emergent Englishes, or the freedom of use that so characterises the global lingua franca, but in enhancing the abilities of native speakers to approach them in more fruitful and constructive ways.

English in the European Union

English is one of the 11 official languages of the EU. However, it remains a bone of contention. Generally, it is spoken by at least 55 per cent of EU citizens. Within the EU, English use is led by younger European parliamentarians. However, older generations grew up at a time at which French dominated. Recently, there has been a shift in EU practice: all documents are now drafted in English. In part, this reflects the concerns of new members like Austria, Finland, Sweden and, before them, Ireland. However, it also reflects the prevalence of English more generally.

In the words of one EU professional, the result is a 'pidgin technocratic form of English'. Figures can be 'degressive' (gradually decreasing in rate on sums below a certain level), meetings cluttered with 'commentology' (the decision-making procedure of a committee-based system) and, reflecting francophone influence on the English patois, interns are 'stageaires'. On the one hand, this combination of general fluency and particular idiom undermines the advantage that native speakers might have in EU debates. On the other, it illustrates how native speakers cannot assume that they will be able to operate easily in English-speaking environments.

The English spoken is particular to the EU; it is a common denominator. David Crystal speaks of it as an 'interlingua': in cases in which there is a no translator available to mediate between two languages, English is the most commonly spoken substitute – 'Euro-English'.[146] This interlingua is owned not by the native English speakers of the parliament, but by the parliament itself.

Other lingua francas?

Niall Ferguson's observation that 'the old monopolies on which power was traditionally based – monopolies on wealth, political office and knowledge – have in large measure broken up'[147] heralds an important lesson with regard to languages and the status of English. In the changing world we must look far beyond our relationship with fellow English speakers, native or otherwise. Although English continues to be the language of choice, there are signs that other languages have equal, if not greater, appeal. When international cooperation is sought, but there is no common language, there is diminishing reason to assume that English will be chosen as a common platform for communication.

> *Investment by language provision: Chinese language training in Sudan*
>
> China has become Sudan's largest inward investor. With a 40 per cent stake in Sudan's oil industry it has financed part of a major economic boom. About a third of the oil-rich African nation's

annual production is exported to China. The cash that this pumps into a controversial regime has caused international concern. It is also revealing in linguistic terms. Initially, the language barrier posed a problem. However, the Chinese are seeking to overcome this by developing language teaching in Sudan and other African countries, in part through the government-sponsored Confucius Institutes.[148]

This is an important lesson to those who think that the English language will remain a passport to business. At first, the Chinese and Sudanese faced mutual incomprehension: the solution found was that Mandarin, rather than English, would be the language used. Joshua Kurlantzick, writing for the Carnegie Endowment for International Peace, a leading US think tank, has pointed out that 'Beijing offers African nations an alternate consumer for resources, a model of successful development, and trade policies that can be more benign than western initiatives'.[149] With the money, success and interest coming from China, why should the Sudanese and others learn English rather than Mandarin? When it comes to language choice, economics can be a stronger force than the appeal of what has hitherto been the world's lingua franca.

As other languages catch up, English is also losing its global purchase. Looking back at the story of power, it is for this reason that English might be less dominant in the future than it has been in the past. Power hasn't disappeared, but its loyalty has shifted. Around the world, the rising nations are not native English speakers, but speakers of other languages and, in particular, Hindi, Mandarin and Urdu. At the moment, English serves people's purposes well, but in the future, this is less likely to be the case. Concentrating solely on the advantages that English offers in emerging markets now is to ignore the importance of learning the skills to participate in those markets at a later point. In the UK, by focusing on the multinationals' success in the age of capitalism, we are in danger of undermining our competitiveness in the age of Languages 2.0.

In a twenty-first-century twist on the nationalistic debates of past centuries, current global politics would seem to accelerate this trend. Growing resentment of the US and US influence, in particular, has led people to associate it with aspects of politics, society and culture that they choose to reject and avoid. Unsurprisingly, according to the US polling house, Pew International, the decline in opinion of the US is particularly apparent in Islamic countries.[150] Further opinion polls in South East Asia show that people look forward to the withdrawal of US influence: as a result, many young people are learning Chinese.[151]

In global political terms, this reflects a shift of huge importance. In Africa, the uptake of Mandarin is driven by more than Sudanese economic pragmatism. Three years ago, announcements at Nairobi's Jomo Kenyatta International Airport were made in English and Kiswahili: now they are made in Chinese as well.[152] For fellow developing countries, China represents an attractive role model, especially in economic terms.[153] Speaking to the UK foreign policy organisation, Chatham House, Elizabeth Sidiropoulos, director of the South African Institute of International Affairs, outlined the reasons for China's appeal to African nations. It brings no colonial baggage, and emphasises south–south relationships. China speaks to Africa from a different continent, but from the same world. Still more revealingly, 'China is attractive to African states because it is seen as contributing to the end of western dominance and uni-polarity'.[154] The dynamics to which she refers do not just reflect the emerging nature of power, they stand in pointed rejection to older imperial models. Nevertheless, it is unfair and naïve to read threat into the growing interest of African countries in China. India, for example, was mining in Zambia well before Chinese involvement with the country; still, the point remains that China and the Chinese language are real rivals in terms of appeal.

Within China itself, the allure of MTV, the BBC and others is great and this has encouraged enhanced interaction. While the broadcast of foreign media is still heavily monitored and restricted, increasingly content is available online. Although this remains a regulated space in China, it is also much more difficult to control. The media giant

Viacom recently struck a deal with Baidu, one of China's biggest and fastest-growing internet providers and the fourth most visited website in the world; the deal has enabled MTV to be shown for the first time to mainstream China.[155] One consequence is that China is becoming less isolated and so more attractive to foreign students and learners of Chinese. In an interview for the *New York Times*, Jessie Yak, a young Singaporean who went to Beijing to study Chinese, said: 'People looked down on China, now there is a 180-degree change. In the past, experience in the United States was important; now experience in China is just as good.'[156]

Just like Jessie, Western business and enterprise is also focusing on China; 61.8 per cent of transnational corporations see it as the most attractive prospective location for research and development work. The next most popular venue is the US, with 41.2 per cent and then India with 29.4 per cent.[157] The UK, in particular, has a vested interest in continued economic involvement with China: by the end of 2005, there were 4891 British-invested projects there with a realised value of US$13.2 billion, and a further US$10.8 billion contracted.[158] Mandarin is seeing an equal bloom. Already the most spoken language on the planet, it is showing no sign of stopping. By the time of the last US census in 2000, Chinese had leaped from fifth to second place as the country's most widely spoken language after English.[159] This appeal is not lost on the Chinese government, which seeks to quadruple the number of foreign learners of Mandarin to 100 million by 2010.

Where, in the eighteenth and nineteenth centuries, English represented the route to power, in the twenty-first, it could well lose that crown to Mandarin. It is not that English will lose its influence, it is rather that speaking solely English, and failure to adapt to different Englishes, will no longer be adequate. As a result, the benefits that the UK gets from English will be rapidly diminished. In the nineteenth century, as Lord Macaulay's minute demonstrated, Britain's response was directive action. Now, in the age of the citizen and 'Language 2.0', things will have to be very different.

7. Learning from elsewhere

Framing policy

Major, standardised languages have at least some control over their own evolution, and those that are supported by a government have ways of steering their relations among the other languages with which they are linked by communication, competition, cooperation and conflict.

Jean Laponce, Professor Emeritus,
University of British Columbia[160]

'A social cataclysm in the process of happening?'

In language planning and policy for the future, the UK government must be aware of trends like the nationalism that has risen in Bengalooru. On the one hand, the promotion of English can cause resentment; on the other, the UK must understand the impact of protectionist measures taken on behalf of languages by other governments. As Renault's adoption of English demonstrates, protectionist measures by nation states rarely overcome economic forces. The anthropologist Clifford Geertz saw a major threat in this linguistic dilemma:

The tension between these two impulses – to move with the tide of the present and to hold to an inherited course – gives new state nationalism its peculiar air of being at once hell-bent toward modernity and morally outraged by its manifestations.

> *There is a certain irrationality in this. But it is more than a collective derangement: it is a social cataclysm in the process of happening.*[161]

Policy that responds to global English must be framed in ways that meet direct needs, but are also more sensitive to given contexts. The interests of users and official bodies and the UK itself are not mutually exclusive. Nevertheless, the different ways in which the English language is of value to learners globally and in the UK mean that different approaches are needed in different contexts. In some areas, these entail greater control and precise action by government and other organisational bodies, like the British Council; in others, a more hands-off approach is required.

Language use, and in particular the choice to use the English language, can be driven by several concerns, which are listed below. As descriptions of precise activities, these overlap, but they do act as guides to the different options that are available to government and others in seeking to create coherent policy in relation to the English language.

- **The steer of market forces:** because English offers significant business opportunities, it is driven by an invisible hand. However, that is unlikely to last and, as English grows as a second language, the strength of multilingualism in that marketplace means that there is an imperative to address the language skills of the UK.[162]
- **The individual interest in the language:** the choice of a given language is driven by the values associated with it by a given user, and so is shaped by the values and interests that those users bring to the language.
- **The need for a common medium of communication:** because there is a need for common ground and understanding, there is a need for public negotiation of meaning within a de facto lingua franca. In certain areas, this will require central control.

○   *Governmental interest in the English language:* the UK
   has a vested interest in the strength of English – financial
   interest and the maintenance of influence and access to
   innovation will require language policies that reflect
   changes in English and a changed attitude to ownership
   that we see reflected in the way that people around the
   world use languages.

These areas provide a way of thinking about how to balance the need
to maintain the benefits that the UK accrues from the English
language and the growing independence of use that is evident around
the world. Government departments must develop responses to
changes in global English that are appropriate to the contexts of their
particular policy areas.

Figure 9 provides a framework within which to think about
activities and policies in relation to the English language. It deals with
intention, rather than effect, and, as before, the interests are not
mutually exclusive. So, to take a very common example, the decision
to translate and publish a book in English represents the power of
market forces: the author and publisher may decide that the English
language is the medium through which influence might be achieved
or profit can be gained. The decision of an individual to learn English
so that they can read books like this would be driven by personal
interest in accessing a widespread source of knowledge.

As well as helping to describe the nature of the activities related to
the English language, it helps to see how effects and developments can
best be approached in the future.

Four approaches
The steer of market forces: the invisible hand

Learners around the world will always sail with the prevailing
commercial wind, in this case using English. It gives access to markets
and it gives access to knowledge. However, UK policy-makers need to
be aware of major cross-winds that we can forecast for the future.
Mandarin, in particular, is likely to hold as much appeal for a

Figure 9 Approaches to shaping language policy

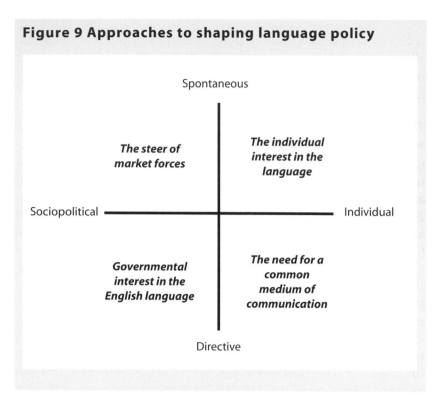

Spontaneous

The steer of market forces

The individual interest in the language

Sociopolitical — — Individual

Governmental interest in the English language

The need for a common medium of communication

Directive

developing nation as does English. We cannot assume that the appeal of English will be uncontested for long.

In science and technology, there will be a growing imperative to access Chinese and other knowledge sources, and to collaborate with innovators from these regions.[163] Domestically, as the multi-lingualism of the UK develops, we will need to provide services in a wider range of languages. This is already happening in some public services, but others, both private and public, should do the same. Like the signs in Miami Dade County Jail and outside the Library of Congress, a more locally sensitive approach to public information will be necessary. Multilingualism is an asset, but it is also a challenge and a public service in its own right. In the private sector, like the US banks, providers will have to offer multilingual services.

Already, there are instances across the UK in which this sensitivity is becoming visible. However, policy-makers and private interests in all areas must learn to read the movements of this invisible hand relative to their particular concerns. This applies for both global English and domestic multilingualism.

The individual interest in the language: learning from open source software

Open source software has revolutionised spheres from the internet to information. Wikipedia, its most well-known exponent, continues to attract a huge community of users and has, since its inception in 2000, grown to challenge developed and respected sources of knowledge like *Encyclopaedia Britannica*. In the pamphlet *Wide Open*, Geoff Mulgan, Tom Steinberg and Omar Salem examined the implications of open source methods. Open source software is 'any computer software distributed under a license which allows users to change or share the software's source code'. It offers 'alternative methods of validation, improvement and knowledge sharing to those currently used by the professionals, policy-makers, universities and media organisations'.[164] In suggesting its application to other paths of innovation, they recommend that it 'should not be stretched too loosely to cover new areas', but that three broad headings cover other applications of the same ideas:

O   open knowledge
O   open team working
O   open conversations.

What are the implications of looking at the English language through this lens? Like the programs of open source software, the English language has a 'source code'. David Crystal has concluded that 'there is every likelihood of "core" features of English grammar becoming a major feature of the description of New Englishes, as time goes by'.[165] Like Wikipedia, people can use this core in varying ways that represent the diversity of the English language.

Seeing the development of English in these terms allows us to recognise the individuality implicit in language choice and use. It also enables a more democratic basis for language planning. In certain contexts, providing learners with a linguistic core will enable them to contribute far more to the global pool of knowledge that English represents. Taking the headings used in *Wide Open*, the potential of viewing language through an open source framework becomes clear:

○ **Open knowledge** is derived from the widespread use and enrichment of English. Just as the language benefited from words invented to describe and navigate the New World, so new usage by different cultures around the world have stimulated the development of the English language in new directions. We need to provide learners, both at home and abroad, with more efficient ways of accessing this very open source of development.

○ **Open team working** is a means by which to help learners access new developments in English. Language growth can ossify when it is retained in fixed communities of interest; it can become impenetrable to outsiders. As jargon and the 'unspeak' of which Stephen Poole has written demonstrate, this is possible even within the same language.[166] However, to use, for a moment, some contemporary jargon, languages are the ultimate example of public goods that are co-produced. They develop by human interaction. If policy is to take this approach, then it is necessary that there is equal input into the language by those who will use it.

○ **Open conversations** are the means by which this can work. The internet is a forum in which different uses of the English language can co-exist and can be brought together millions of times each day. On one level, this illustrates the importance of shifting our perception of the language to a more open source model. On another, it indicates the potential of using this forum in language provision and in developing the accommodation skills of native speakers of English.

Open source techniques offer great potential for language provision and planning for language development. Online consultation forums, for example, can provide a means of aggregating a more democratic and globally accepted norm in contexts where standardisation is required. More generally, open source thinking provides a framework within which to see language development. Policy-makers must in the future be aware of the democratic elements and public ownership of the English language.

The need for a common medium of communication: the English language as a public space

First launched in the UK in November 2003, Webplay (www.webplay.org) is an 'internet-based project that enables primary schoolchildren from contrasting areas to work with a professional theatre company to create, produce and perform short plays'.[167] It used the format of a common project to bring together schoolchildren from different areas and so share their outlooks, opinions and experience. Initially, the project was run between urban and rural schools in the Midlands and focused on the English, literacy, ICT and drama aspects of the National Curriculum. In the next phase, links were developed with a school in Los Angeles. The children soon became interested in the international connections they could access and the different experiences they could share. The comparisons they made were about far more than the differences between US and UK culture. Even in partnerships between the UK schools, pupils from the rural school were surprised to discover that 18 languages other than English were spoken as a first language in their urban counterpart.

Online partnerships indicate an important role for websites that enable young people from different linguistic backgrounds and cultures to communicate with English speakers from around the world. This would bring young people into contact with different attitudes and outlooks as well as different Englishes. It would also help foreign learners develop their language skills.

In line with the more open approach to language outlined above, we need to develop the concept of English as a shared public space. The value of English as global lingua franca is in part in the interactions, encounters and conversations that it enables. Policy relating to public space suggests ways in which language policy might address particular interests, such as the diversification of a language in which there is common ownership:

> *One policy response . . . is the effort to promote public space as an economic asset worthy of private and commercial investment. This investment can reinforce private control of previously public spaces, but it can also encourage recognition that the degree of welcome and accessibility found by diverse visitors contributes to the economic vitality of a particular place.*[168]

We must encourage collaborations like Webplay to enable learners and users to explore the English language and understand and come to grips with the common ownership of it that we have. The incentive for government and private companies to invest in this area is in building our capacity to draw value from a world in which very different linguistic and cultural values can come into regular and everyday contact.

Governmental interest: the Confucian way

Directive policies can work, but in specific contexts. In Virginia, efforts to standardise police radio-speak met with consternation. The use of '10-codes' to designate specific situations developed in the 1920s. As different police divisions emerged across the US, this language evolved to mean different things in different areas. However, when – as happened on 11 September 2001 – police officials from different areas have suddenly to cooperate, confusion can reign. In Alexandria (VA), for instance, '10-54' refers to a breathalyser; for Virginia State police, it means 'livestock on the highway'. In cases like this, where standardisation is necesssary, centralised action and authority will be necessary.[169]

There are also examples in which languages are actively promoted. The Académie Française has already been mentioned and, in the Alliance Française, France has an organisation overseas that promotes the language and culture. Similarly, Germany has the Goethe Institute; Spain, the Cervantes Institutes; and the UK, the British Council. One in particular, however, is worth closer attention.

The Chinese government recently announced that about 30 million people around the world are studying Mandarin. As we have seen, Beijing hopes to increase this to 100 million over the next few years. In pursuing this goal, it has developed and funded Confucius Institutes, which were conceptualised in 2004. Run by the Chinese National Office for Teaching Chinese as a Foreign Language, the Hanban, these are offices around the world for the teaching of Chinese language and culture. Some 80 Confucius Institutes have opened in 36 countries around the world. Currently, they exist in several countries including Australia, Japan, Sweden and the US. Reflecting the growing interest of Chinese in Africa, the first Confucius Institute opened there in June 2004.[170] In the UK, there are Institutes at the Universities of Edinburgh and Manchester and the School of Oriental and African Studies. Soon, an Institute specifically for business will open at the London School of Economics in partnership with HSBC.

This final association reveals the basis of their appeal: the growing awareness of China's importance and power, especially in economic terms. According to Robert Davis, the director of the Chicago Confucius Institute, business owners in even traditionally Cantonese areas of the city are learning Mandarin, and there is now a waiting list for schools seeking to work with the Institute.[171] Although they are based on models provided by organisations like the British Council, Confucius Institutes differ because they explicitly link language policy to national interest and promotion. The strategy behind them is to house Institutes within universities.

As commentators writing in the *Asia Times* put it, 'the potential to use the institutes for the long-term building of Chinese soft-power influence' is clear.[172] A Chinese professor of international relations at a prominent Beijing university put this still more clearly: 'The economic and industrial threat that China is perceived to be could be abated by the communication of Chinese values overseas – this could easily be achieved through language teaching.'[173] Diplomatically, Confucius Institutes play to a shift in global attention in terms that respond to market concerns. As the importance of China in economic terms grows, so does the attraction of the Chinese language. In addition to the Confucius Institutes, the Hanban is selecting, training and providing living expenses for hundreds of Chinese volunteers to teach Mandarin in 23 different countries: in 2005, there were 10,000 volunteers waiting for placements.[174]

The drive to promote Mandarin makes for interesting reading. Using language providers in ways so directly associated with national interest is not an option for the UK. First, the UK does not have the same exclusive association with the English language as does China with Mandarin at the moment; second, English is a global public good and cannot be exploited in such nationalistic and commercialised terms.

However, the model of association with universities is attractive especially with regard to sector-specific concerns such as those of the Office of Science and Innovation (OSI). In some areas language policy is legitimate, such as maintaining safety and standards in a given area of international cooperation, or supplying language training where there is an existing demand, for example in technological and scientific institutes. Furthermore, there is also an opportunity to connect English language provision with UK enterprise and initiatives overseas. In this, we could again follow the Chinese lead, where the diaspora contributes an estimated 40 per cent of investment capital to mainland China and the promotion of Mandarin connects with these communities.[175] As the UK's diaspora increases, we should consider what similar opportunities might arise.

8. Some key skills for the future

We have argued that the changes already under way in global English are part of the bigger story of our future, and that languages and language policy are an essential part of preparing for that. Policy-makers must put the issues raised by global English at the heart of education. We have suggested a framework through which to approach language policy. But we also need to address the skills people will need to navigate the linguistic landscape of the future, and function as global citizens, collaborating and cooperating in an increasingly global context.

Language skills

The days when those whose first tongue is English could ignore the need to speak other languages are over. The bonus of ordering a burger in English while on holiday will increasingly seem fairly paltry in comparison with the economic and cultural penalties of monolingualism. Certainly those who are monolingual have always 'missed out' in many senses, but global English is making this increasingly so.

Alongside the push and pull factors that drive the uptake of English across the world, new, equally forceful drivers are making the UK's poor linguistic competence unsustainable. It is true that getting children to learn languages *earlier* is key, building aptitude and liking for language study, but offering the choice at 14 to drop languages is too close in character to how the UK currently thinks of foreign-language learning: as a choice and an added extra to the fundamentals of education.

This must be addressed. More than ever before, language skills are a core competency and not a luxury. Multilingualism should no longer be the marker of sophistication. Instead, it must become a reality of the UK's skills set and government and others must cooperate to motivate young people to learn different languages. This may take additional focus and effort, but the opportunity cost of failing to address the language skills problem grows as each day passes.

Cultural literacy

Our society is multicultural and our world is one of many cultures. The problem is that there is a global difficulty in *reading* other cultures. Our newspapers, media and websites herald numerous stories of insecurity and, worse still, hostility. In January 2007, this reached almost crisis point when Jade Goody's behaviour in the Big Brother House towards a fellow contestant, Bollywood actress Shilpa Shetty, caused outrage in India and national embarrassment for the UK. In response, on 25 January, calls were made for the more efficient teaching of Britishness in our schools.[176] However, this misses a fundamental horror: the opinions expressed by Jade Goody *are* an element of Britishness today. It is rooted in a fundamental lack of skills to relate to people of other cultures.

Controversially, Samuel Huntingdon has described this situation as being a 'clash of civilisations'.[177] This seems almost a self-fulfilling prophecy as we pay less attention to reading difference and more to observing it. There is a strong motivation and policy need to overcome such negativity and to promote understanding in its place. However, there has been insufficient examination of just how we can reach that understanding. More than ever before, we are travelling, seeing and encountering for ourselves the culture and heritage of our neighbours and fellows. Language is a key means by which we do this. Using new technology, we can access words, texts and literature from all over the world. Nightly, travel and documentary programmes bring sights, words and symbols from afar to our screens. The challenge that faces us is how we move beyond seeing such hybrid languages as Chinglish, Hinglish, Singlish, Spanglish and multiple others as amusing corruptions. We should see them as varieties, rather than 'interlanguages', which bring with them their own distinct culture and provide equally distinct means of understanding their users. The linguistic expert Barbara Seidlhofer has pointed to the 'tenacious deficit view of ELF in which variation is perceived as deviation' and only recently has ESOL scholarship itself come to recognise this more democratic point of view.[178] The growing need for enhanced skills in cultural literacy make it essential that this thinking is reflected in wider policy.

Beyond the staples of reading, writing and arithmetic, the challenge is to think afresh about what skills we need in a changing and hyper-connected world. Cultural literacy should be incorporated more surely into language learning in ways that reflect the real need to develop the skills with which we can read and approach other cultures.

Cultural literacy can also be developed by the way that English is taught as a foreign or second language. Domestically and overseas, it must be taught in ways that help users to express and articulate their values. In a world of increased global communication, there is the real opportunity for English-language learning to draw people of different experiences together.

Accommodation

Jennifer Jenkins, a linguistics expert at King's College London, has written that 'English is still taught as though the primary need of learners is to be able to communicate with its native speakers, and with the assumption that correct English is either Standard British or American English'.[179] From the point of view of English language providers, the responsibility is for native speakers of English to adapt to a 'smaller world' in which they will encounter multiple forms of the language.

Alongside skills in other languages, it is essential that we develop the skills to interpret and respond to speakers of the different Englishes that we will encounter increasingly often in the future. Learning foreign languages helps develop sensitivity to the difficulties that non-native speakers can have. Accommodation skills must comprise both an understanding of different Englishes and a more nuanced understanding of what it is like to be a non-native speaker. Current thinking among scholars of linguistics suggests that ELF has developed to occupy a specific place, alternatively called a 'third space', a 'third culture' or a 'third place'.[180] Difference from English as it is spoken by native speakers, or those who have learned it as a foreign language, is not explained by legitimacy or imposed standards of 'correctness'. As the English spoken around the world becomes more distant from that spoken in Westminster, Washington, Wisconsin or Winchester, so we need to help native speakers of the future to develop the skill of *accommodating* to new usage of the language.

9. Shaping policy for a world of global English

Recommendations

While many around the world use English to pursue individual opportunity, many of the assumptions that surround it either assume authority that is no longer valid, or reinforce existing inequalities. Government policy cannot just be about helping people to learn English across the world. There needs to be recognition that people learn the language in their own terms and to their own ends and these do not necessarily relate to the UK or any other country of which English is the mother tongue.

Policies must be sensitive to a global population of English speakers. English is more a family of languages than a single language with set rules and orthodoxies. Although this is understood on occasion, this single fact must be at the root of UK policy thinking in a range of areas. This must be reflected in putting policy into action. English must be studied and used contextually, rather than in the generalist manner that can too often dominate. Its changing nature will affect all government departments because it affects all walks of life. Our basic recommendations are therefore that:

○ **all government departments should develop a language strategy to look at the importance of changes in global English and the growth of other languages in their areas of concern**

○ and, in line with this, **English language provision should**

meet the needs of learners in specific areas and in terms that concentrate on communicative ability, rather than fulfilling demands that others have of them.

Policy must also respond to the different considerations that this pamphlet has uncovered. Our recommendations follow the different approaches to language policy outlined in chapter 7. In line with this framework, they are presented in ways that speak to different audiences and are mutually supportive. So, directive action in one area might also provide the opportunities for individuals around the world to pursue their own ends.

In each section, the recommendations comprise two parts. First, a general point on the tenor and nature of policy that they describe and, second, specific action points that should be taken.

The individual interest in the language

In addition to developing the skills outlined in the previous chapter, one of the main findings is that English is adopted in different contexts for purposes that are driven by individual needs. There is an imperative to understand these needs in the given contexts in which English is learned and used.

○ *Individual needs and contexts must be reflected in ESOL teaching in the UK:* English language learners in the UK bring different experiences and different attitudes. These must be at the heart of their studies with provision following a more personalised approach. That would give learners the chance to shape their own linguistic development by working with them to articulate best practice. At the moment, the focus is too much on fulfilling the UK's needs in terms of capacity. The Skills for Life agenda, and much of the debate around citizenship, focus primarily on the functions demanded of learners, rather than the enabling and communicative skills that would suit them best. Learners in the UK should be taught skills of integration – basic, functional language skills – and the skills to contribute their own experiences. Citizenship requirements for English language abilities should be framed in terms of personalised potential, rather than purely the UK's requirements.

○ *Creating a taskforce for English language teachers:* Language teachers are often the first and closest point of contact between the newcomer and the UK and policy-makers should consult them with a view to integrating the individual and the needs that they bring into language planning. They should therefore be included more comprehensively in the policy-making process. A taskforce should be developed, using the expertise of language teachers to advise policy-makers and build a new strategy for personalised language learning.

○ *Developing context-specific teaching in the UK:* Overseas, context-based English language training text books and teaching materials are already in place. Working with the taskforce outlined above, government should follow a similar practice in the UK and ensure that there is no blanket solution to teaching in the UK and context-based teaching materials are developed accordingly.

The steer of market forces

Learning English provides an easy access route into global markets, and much of the uptake of English around the world is a response to these forces, driven by an 'invisible hand'. Understanding this context and the emerging threats of other languages, particularly Mandarin, to this situation will be essential to shaping policy. How English fits with global markets and trends, like the rise of migration among UK citizens, will also be central to language policy in the future.

○ *Re-engaging with the UK diaspora as 'English language ambassadors':* Great interest in learning English around the world coincides with a rise in UK citizens moving abroad. Government should seek to re-engage with this diaspora community and simultaneously build links overseas. One option is that the UK works with these communities in 'ambassadorial' capacities, with learning providers in their new environments to communicate knowledge and understanding of the UK and provide bridging roles with the cultures in which they are immersed and from which learners come. To do this, training should be provided to providers and expat 'ambassadors' to accommodate the values that learners and their languages bring.

○ **_Providing English language training in developing contexts:_** English empowers people seeking commercial opportunity, but there is a developmental need to provide the further opportunity for people to use skills in English. The Department for International Development should engage with learners and providers to deliver context-appropriate English language training as part of an aid package where appropriate. Following the individual nature of language need, this should be done in close alignment with development organisations, language providers and, most of all, the learners themselves. Pursuing multilingual strategies will help to preserve and protect other languages.

○ **_Re-evaluating the potential of specialist English language ambassadors:_** English is readily understood and used all over the world. It therefore represents a significant opportunity for public diplomacy. By developing a series of 'English language ambassadors' from specific fields, the government could build on this appeal to create links around the world. Specialists, for example from the cultural and scientific industries, already have established contacts and companies are very active in teaching their staff English, or local languages.

Government should encourage collaboration between these people and organisations, and learning professionals and organisations like the British Council to develop English language teaching specific to their fields. Equally, the English language training industry is an active and established point of contact across the world: organisations within that field should collaborate to reconsider the ambassadorial role that they might play. At the same time, government should fund English speakers from around the world to travel to the UK to build links, understanding and cultural literacy within the UK.

The need for a common medium of communication

The common means of communication that the English language offers could bring advantage both to the UK and in global terms. To make the most of this opportunity, we need to develop skills that reflect the diversity that there is within English. It is also necessary to prepare schoolchildren in the UK with the means to work confidently and competently in a global marketplace in which multilingualism will be a necessity.

○ *Developing cultural literacy:* Cultural literacy will be a vital skill in an increasingly globalised and integrated world. As we encounter different cultures, speakers of other languages and speakers of different forms of language, we will need the skills to accommodate and identify the different perspectives that they bring. In the UK, language training should incorporate these skills. We should also develop programmes in which foreign language learners of English can learn by contributing their own cultural experience and backgrounds to UK schoolchildren and citizens.

○ *Developing pupil-led exchange for the information age:* The spread of digital technologies and communication provides a means of accessing and encountering languages and the cultures that they represent far more frequently than ever before. Education providers need to work with this trend and develop links between learners of English at all levels across the world. Fostering dialogue with learners of different kinds of English in classrooms around the world will give young people and older learners the chance to encounter different cultures and develop the skills and awareness necessary to accommodate them. One way of doing this would be to incorporate 'classroom links' into the curriculum, encouraging communication between languages and across borders, giving pupils and learners experience of different outlooks on similar issues.

○ *Reinventing traditional pupil exchange:* Pupil exchanges have long been part of our education system and motivation for uptake should be developed. However, their overall impact is limited both by whether or not a school offers the opportunity and a low uptake. Initially, schools should work with parents and pupils to encourage exchanges on a more personalised basis – exchanges should be particular to the pupil's preference. However, government should also support schemes that build exchange into learning. In higher education, language students at university are expected to spend a year abroad in an environment in which the language they study is spoken. Respective government departments should collaborate with the Department for Education and Skills (DfES) to support and fund the opportunity for students of other subjects to learn an appropriate language and study their subject in an appropriate country. For example, as China, India, Korea and other countries become more important innovators in science, so the OSI should work with the DfES to fund exchange schemes; similarly, engineering exchanges could be developed with Germany. Earlier in the education system, an awareness of the languages necessary to specific subjects should be factored into the education system. For example, students of design at GCSE should develop skills in Italian, students of engineering, Mandarin and German. Similarly, respective governmental departments should fund and support exchange schemes to bring foreign learners to the UK, and give UK learners the chance to experience the workings of different subjects and specialisms in another language.

○   *Reinventing the British Council as a 'public space':*
Around the world, the British Council is a recognised space for finding out about and accessing English language training. Government should fund the British Council to develop more consistently as a 'public space' for the English language. As well as providing information for learners, the offices should also be developed as a forum in which learners can contribute their own experiences, developing to a network of different Englishes. Two possible methods for helping this happen are:

1.   *Connecting learning centres:* Creating a user-based intranet between the Council's offices would provide a learning tool capable of reflecting the differences that there are within global English. This would also create a space in which learners could interact and so it would be attractive to individual learners as a good means to access information and opportunities in its own right.

2.   *Developing a scheme for global scholarships:* Once these opportunities are created, there is a real need for the UK government to back them up with support to develop them into links between the UK and the rest of the world, bringing cultural experience and new links and developing the 'English language ambassadors' mentioned above. A small percentage of money from the

profits that Council offices around the world make from English language training could go into a central pot to facilitate exchange. This could be used to support foreign language students in the UK to travel overseas, and ESOL students to travel to the UK. Distribution of these 'English language scholarships' could be determined according to the demand in each area. So, the amount contributed by one office would correlate to the number of scholarships it has to offer; equally, the nature of the scholarships that it offers would correlate to the needs of the learners for whom it caters.

○ **_Fostering scientific exchange:_** Science and innovation, in particular, are areas in which the UK needs to work to maintain its interests. But here, also, the story is one of potential for and of collaboration. The OSI and the DfES should work together to support UK students studying scientific and technological subjects to develop the language skills and cultural experience that will enable them to cooperate with innovators overseas in countries like China, India and Korea. In *The Atlas of Ideas*, Demos argued that 'scholarships and exchanges will remain critical as a way of strengthening collaborative networks. The Royal Society's idea for scholarships, which we suggest should be called "Darwin Scholarships" to coincide with the 200th anniversary of Darwin's birth in 2009, could provide for 200 places given to postdoctoral and mid-career scientists for collaboration overseas.'[181] A similar scheme, at an earlier stage of scientific advancement, should include language training specific to their areas of study.

Governmental action

This pamphlet has argued that language policy has ultimately to respect individual choice and context, and there is an overriding need to avoid a doctrinaire approach that stipulates set rules. Precise actions that enable individual benefit and respond to market forces are dealt with above. However, at the same time, government and others do need to take action to preserve their interests.

○ *Involving new learners of English in the UK:* As newcomers to the UK develop language skills, part of their learning should incorporate the opportunity to visit schools in the UK, teaching pupils about their own languages and cultures. Clearly, this would be subject to existing demands and rules relating to adult visitors to schools; however, this is an opportunity and resource to build skills in cultural literacy that should not be missed.

○ *Starting language lessons early and building motivation to study languages:* Language lessons should begin in schools from an early age and language learning should be motivated in the more personalised ways discussed above. We learn and adapt to languages best when we are young and this aptitude should be developed and nurtured. Some schools are already offering Mandarin and this should be available to all. Working with some of the mechanisms mentioned above, for example the new communicative opportunities created by the internet, government should investigate ways to diversify the curriculum, building skills in different languages. The DfES's 'languages ladder', which takes an asset-based approach to learning, is a step in the right direction. Learners, from an early age, are now able to assess and channel their own progress according to their own ambitions with regard to the language they are learning. The same model could be applied later (eg at GCSE level) and in line with the cross-departmental activity recommended by this pamphlet, enabling learners to progress according to their own preference in the areas of their interest. Government should investigate the opportunities that global English and educational partnerships of the sort discussed above can provide for more specific learning based on the interests and other choices of the child. The curriculum for other subjects, like the sciences, could include language components taught in association with language teachers and providers.

○ ***Developing skills in accommodation:*** Schools in the UK must also teach skills in accommodation. As more and more of us encounter different forms of English, both online and off, it is essential that we can adapt to them and approach them as different forms of the language. Within schools the English curriculum should incorporate these skills and government should fund the proposals mentioned above, such as online exchange, for building young people's exposure to different forms of English. Putting the work of Meera Syal on the curriculum represents a major step in encouraging this.

○ ***Developing a learning network for global English:*** Constraints on funding have forced the British Council to close libraries around the world. These should be reinvigorated as nodal points of a global network of the English language as part of the 'public space' of British Council offices. The Foreign and Commonwealth Office and the Department for Culture Media and Sport should support the development of the Council's offices as public spaces that provide learners with access to a digital network. This could then be related to educational provision in the UK in the ways discussed above.

○ ***London speaks with the world:*** Demos author Charlie Tims recently wrote of the Olympics as 'the biggest learning opportunity on earth'.[182] In 2008, Beijing is using the Olympics to develop language skills that will be both a tool of public diplomacy during the Games themselves, and a means of developing vital English language skills for the future. London has the chance to go one better and use the Olympiad prior to 2012 and the Games themselves to develop skills in language and accommodation and to demonstrate an understanding of the UK's new position in the world. This will be both a means of managing the Games more smoothly, and a means of driving foreign language uptake in the UK. A multilingual Olympiad would be a vital step in redressing the impact of the Anglophone image that the UK can have overseas, such as that expressed by the foreign ambassadors to the UK mentioned in this pamphlet. 'Beijing speaks English' should become 'London speaks with the world'.

Democtionary.org

This pamphlet has outlined the shift in how English is spread, from imposition to appropriation. Global English is best understood no longer as a language, but as a family of languages. Each manifests cultural experiences that speak of a changing relationship between the UK and the rest of the world. In line with the shift to 'Languages 2.0', this could be mapped using a website that tracks and provides a visual representation of English across the globe. We call this 'democtionary.org'.

This would be an open dictionary-style resource to which people could add entries from all over the world. Each entry would be 'tagged', providing geographical information. So, for example, 'robot' could be tagged as an automaton in the UK, and in its South African usage as a traffic light. Equally, new words could be contributed as they are used and come into recognition from whatever part of the world. The features of web 2.0 allow the data and information to be mapped on to others; so for example, the geographical 'tags' could be mixed with Google Earth to visualise the changing landscape of the English language.

Democtionary would be a useful educational tool and, by opening up the record of the lexicon of global English, could provide a tangible record of, and a challenge to, how differences in English can be social differentiators. It would provide an organic representation of the topography of power in global English. Just like Google has rendered the changing currents of power, so democtionary.org could serve to embed the democratising potential of a global lingua franca.

Appendix
'Wah! I heard we all now got big big debate'

Wah! I heard we all now got big big debate.
They said future of proper English is at stake.

All because stupid Singlish spoil the market,
want to change now donno whether too late.

Aiyoh! Ang mo hear us talk like that also want to faint.
Even our 'U' graduates speak like Ah Beng, Ah Seng.

Singlish is like rojak, everything throw inside anyhow mix.
Got Malay, Indian, Chinese and English, can give and take.

When you donno something is under table or chair,
you ask loud loud 'Oi! Under where? Under where?'

When you see somebody behave very bad,
you scold him, 'aiyah! Why you so like that?'

When you ended up in a traffic jam, and got stuck,
you complain, 'today, I sai chia kena very chia lat.'

When you warn your kids to be careful all the way,
you tell them, 'careful har, you better don't play-play!'

When you see moon cakes with many egg yolks,
you say, 'wah! This type good to eat, very shiok!'

When your friend mistook his mother for his aunt,
you disturb him, 'alamak! Why you so blur one?'

You write like that in exam you sure liao.
Teacher mark your paper also kee siao.

This kind of standard how to pass?
Wait, you sure kena last in class.

Other people hear you, say you sound silly.
So like that how to become world-class city?

Basically Singlish got good and got bad.
Aiyah! Everything in life is all like that.

Actually Singlish got one bright side.
I am talking about our national plight.

Maybe I must explain to you what I mean.
If you're prepared to hear me, I'll begin.

Other people all say we all got no culture.
All we got is a lot of joint business ventures.

So we got no culture to glue us together.
End up we all like a big bunch of feathers.

Wind blow a bit too strong only we fly away.
Everybody all go their own separate ways.

Now we must play internet otherwise cannot survive.
Next time the only way to make money, or sure to die.

When other countries' influences all enter,
we sure kena affected left, right and centre.

Sekali our Singporean identity all lost until donno go where.
Even Orang-Utan Ah Meng starts thinking like a Polar Bear.

But still must go IT otherwise become swa koo,
only smarter than Ah Meng of the Mandai Zoo.

Wait the whole world go I.T., we still blur as sontong,
next time we all only qualified to sell laksa in Katong.

So got this kind of problem like that how?
Either sit and wait or do something now.

But actually we all got one 'culture' in Singlish.
It's like rice on the table; it is our common dish.

I know this funny 'culture' is not the best around
so we must tahan a bit until a better one is found.

Not all the time can marry the best man,
so bo pian got no prawns, fish also can.

I donno whether you agree with me or not?
I just simply sharing with you my thoughts.

Singlish is just like the garden weeds.
You pull like mad still it would not quit.

Sure got some people like and some do not like.
Singlish and English, they'll still live side by side.[183]

Notes

1   S Coleridge, 'Biographia literaria' in D Stauffer, *Selected Poetry and Prose of Coleridge* (New York: Random House, 1951).
2   N Ferguson, *Empire: How Britain made the modern world* (London: Penguin, 2004).
3   RG Gordon Jr (ed), *Ethnologue: Languages of the world*, 15th edn (Dallas: SIL International, 2005), available at www.ethnologue.com/ (accessed 24 Feb 2007).
4   N Ostler, *Empires of the Word: A language history of the world* (London: Harper Collins, 2006).
5   D Crystal, *English as a Global Language*, 2nd edn (Cambridge: Cambridge University Press, 2003).
6   Ostler, *Empires of the Word*.
7   See www.askoxford.com/concise_oed/linguafranca?view=uk (accessed 25 Feb 2007).
8   Ostler, *Empires of the Word*.
9   This model and that of further development shown in figure 5 are taken from D Graddol, *English Next* (London: British Council, 2006), pdf available at www.britishcouncil.org/learning-research-englishnext.htm (accessed 25 Feb 2007).
10 Crystal, *English as a Global Language*.
11 Ibid.
12 Graddol, *English Next*.
13 O Gibson and A Rattansi, 'Look East', *Guardian*, 13 Nov 2006.
14 N Ferguson, *Colossus: The rise and fall of the American empire* (London: Penguin 2005).
15 Ibid.
16 D Crystal, *The Stories of English* (Harmondsworth: Penguin, 2004).
17 Cited in M Bragg, *The Adventure of English: The biography of a language* (London: Hodder and Stoughton, 2004); the version quoted has been modernised for twenty-first century readers – Caxton's original phrase was 'In

my Iudgemente, the comyn termes that be dayli vsed ben lyghter to be vnderstonde than the olde and auncyent englysshe'.

18   Crystal, *English as a Global Language.*
19   Ibid.
20   Ibid.
21   G Nunberg, 'Will the internet always speak English?', *American Prospect* 11, no 10, 27 Mar to 10 Apr 2000.
22   See http://english.people.com.cn/english/200006/26/eng20000626_43930.html (accessed 25 Feb 2007).
23   Crystal, *English as a Global Language.*
24   S Anholt, *Brand America: The mother of all brands* (London: Cyan, 2004).
25   N Watt and D Gow, 'Chirac vows to fight growing use of English', *Guardian,* 25 Mar 2006.
26   Reported by Reuters, 15 Mar 2006.
27   See www.yourpointofview.com/?WT.mc_id=HBEU_links_Homepage _YPOV_2006/10 (accessed 26 Feb 2007).
28   The data from Forbes is drawn from www.forbes.com/lists/results.jhtml?bktDisplayField=stringfield4&bktDisplayFi eldLength=3&passListId=18&passYear=2004&passListType=Company&search Parameter1=unset&searchParameter2=unset&resultsStart=1&resultsHowMany =100&resultsSortProperties=%2Bstringfield4%2C%2Bnumberfield1&resultsS ortCategoryName=country&passKeyword=&category1=category&category2=c ategory&fromColumnClick=true (accessed 13 Nov 2006).
29   A Sage, 'French toast the English language', *Financial Times,* 25 Jun 2005, see http://business.timesonline.co.uk/tol/business/economics/article537050.ece (accessed 25 Feb 2007).
30   S Baker et al, 'The great English divide', *Business Week,* 13 Aug 2001.
31   A McCue, 'BPO to dominate outsourcing by 2006', *silicon.com,* 4 Feb 2005, see www.silicon.com/research/specialreports/consulting/0,3800004140,39127624,0 0.htm (accessed 25 Feb 2007).
32   J Kynge, *China Shakes the World: The rise of a hungry nation* (London: Wiedenfeld and Nicolson, 2006).
33   Graddol, *English Next.*
34   See the UK Film Council's *Statistical Yearbook 2005/06,* available at www.ukfilmcouncil.org.uk/information/statistics/yearbook/?y=2005&c=1 (accessed 25 Feb 2007).
35   T Jowell, 'Secretary of State's speech to the city', Bloomberg, 14 Mar 2006.
36   These figures are from Bowker, the US ISBN agency, see www.bowker.com/press/bowker/2005_1012_bowker.htm (accessed 25 Feb 2007).
37   J JingJing, 'Found in translation', *China Daily, Business Weekly,* 16 Oct 2006.
38   For further details, see E Edukugho, 'English studies worries don', *Vanguard,* 10 Aug 2006, available at www.vanguardngr.com/articles/2002/features/education/ edu510082006.html (accessed 13 Feb 2007).
39   Ibid.

40   T Friedman, *The World is Flat: A brief history of the twenty-first century* (Harmondsworth: Penguin, 2006).

41   Interview with Demos researcher in Beijing, 12 Oct 2006.

42   Graddol, *English Next*.

43   This data is as of 6 Nov 2006.

44   J Quitney Anderson and L Rainie, *The Future of the Internet II* (Washington DC: Pew Research, 2006).

45   The entire poem is reproduced in the appendix.

46   Quoted in M Warschauer, 'Languages.com: the internet and linguistic pluralism' in I Snyder (ed), *Silicon Literacies: Communication, innovation and education in the electronic age* (London: Routledge, 2002).

47   Quoted in Quitney Anderson and Rainie, *Future of the Internet II*.

48   E Hobsbawm, *Nations and Nationalism since 1780* (Cambridge: Cambridge University Press, 1990).

49   Graddol, *English Next*.

50   Ibid.

51   Ibid.

52   See the Volunteer Service Overseas website at www.vso.org.uk/volunteering/stepone/tefl_teacher.asp (accessed 21 Feb 2007).

53   See http://english.cri.cn/349/2006/01/17/44@43952.htm (accessed 21 Feb 2007).

54   See www.newlaunches.com/archives/nintendo_ds_teaches_english.php# (accessed 21 Feb 2007).

55   See http://forum.skype.com/lofiversion/index.php/t67435.html (accessed 21 Feb 2007).

56   B Kachru, 'English in South Asia' in R Burchfield (ed), *Cambridge History of the English Language*, vol. V, English in Britain and Overseas (Cambridge: Cambridge University Press, 1994), cited in Crystal, *English as a Global Language*.

57   Crystal, *English as a Global Language*.

58   C Achebe, 'English and the African writer', *Transition* 4 (1965), cited in Crystal, *Stories of English*.

59   J Lo Bianco, 'Language planning for globalisation tensions and trends', lecture notes, Prince Phillip Theatre Architecture Building (133), University of Melbourne, 12 Jul 2005, available at www.edfac.unimelb.edu.au/ace/llae/pdfs/lo_bianco_lecture_notes.pdf (accessed 24 Feb 2007).

60   S Wright, *Language Policy and Language Planning* (Basingstoke: Palgrave MacMillan, 2004).

61   Kynge, *China Shakes the World*.

62   N Chapman, 'Rising to the challenge', BBC World Service, *Annual Review 2004/05*, available at www.bbc.co.uk/worldservice/us/annual_review/2004/director.shtml (accessed 28 May 2006).

63   Interview with Demos researcher, 12 Oct 2006.

64   D Crystal, *The Cambridge Encyclopaedia of Language,* 2nd edn (Cambridge: Cambridge University Press, 1998).

65   For further details of *Follow Me,* see http://news.bbc.co.uk/1/hi/programmes/ from_our_own_correspondent/3363077.stm (accessed 24 Feb 2007).

66   Graddol, *English Next.*

67   F Grin, 'L'enseignement des langues etrangères comme politique publique', report to L'Haut Conseil de l'Évaluation de l'École, Paris, Sep 2005, author's translation.

68   Quoted in JingJing, 'Found in translation'.

69   For further details, see the BBC and ippr research, reported in http://news.bbc.co.uk/1/hi/uk/5237236.stm (accessed 25 Feb 2007).

70   T Kirby, 'Britains with second home up 45% in two years', *Independent,* 22 Nov 2006, see http://news.independent.co.uk/uk/this_britain/article2004223.ece (accessed 24 Feb 2007).

71   See http://members.bccthai.com/BCCT/asp/general.asp?MenuItemID= 1&SponsorID=0 (accessed 25 Feb 2007).

72   United Nations World Tourism Organization, *Tourism Highlights,* 2006 edn (Madrid: UNWTO, 2006).

73   Office of National Statistics, *Travel Trends: A report on the 2005 international travel survey* (London: ONS Report, 2006).

74   See www.visitdublin.com/multimedia/iWalk.aspx?id=275 (accessed 25 Feb 2007).

75   'Chinese farmers guide English tour', *People's Daily,* 10 Aug 2000.

76   C Masters, 'France enters crowded English-language news provider', Reuters, 27 Nov 2006).

77   Wright, *Language Policy and Language Planning.*

78   Lord Carter of Coles, *Public Diplomacy Review* (London: Foreign and Commonwealth Office Publication, 2005).

79   Quoted in Crystal, *English as a Global Language.*

80   R King, *Braj Kachru's Asian Englishes* (review article), *World Englishes* 24, no 4 (2005).

81   See S Coughlan, 'It's Hinglish, innit?', BBC, 8 Nov 2006, see http:// news.bbc.co.uk/1/hi/magazine/6122072.stm (accessed 25 Feb 2007).

82   See http://news.bbc.co.uk/1/hi/education/6331869.stm (accessed 6 Feb 2007).

83   Crystal, *English as a Global Language.*

84   Bragg, *Adventure of English.*

85   P Alberch, 'Language in contemporary science: the tool and the cultural icon' in R Chartier and P Corsi (eds), *Sciences et Langues en Europe* (Paris: Editions de l'Ecole des hautes études en sciences sociales, 2006), quoted in Wright, *Language Policy and Language Planning.*

86   See www.newswiretoday.com/news/9919/ (accessed 26 Feb 2007).

87   J Gittings, *The Changing Face of China: From Mao to market* (Oxford: Oxford University Press, 2006).

88   J Laponce, 'Babel and the market: geostrategies for minority languages' in I Maurais and M Morris (eds), *Languages in a Globalising World* (Cambridge: Cambridge University Press, 2004).

89　T Blair, 'The duty to integrate: shared British values', speech at Downing St, 8 Dec 2006, available at www.number-10.gov.uk/output/Page10563.asp (accessed 25 Feb 2007).

90　G Brown, 'We will always strive to be on your side', speech to the Labour Party Conference, Manchester, 25 Sep 2006.

91　S Salman, 'Lost in translation', *Guardian*, 4 Oct 2006, http://society.guardian.co.uk/societyguardian/story/0,,1886566,00.html (accessed 25 Feb 2007).

92　B Rammell, 'English for all', *Guardian*, 10 Oct 2006.

93　National Institute for Adult Continuation in Education, *More than a Language* (Leicester and Cardiff: NIACE, 2006), see www.niace.org.uk/publications/M/MoreThanLanguage.asp (accessed 28 Feb 2007).

94　C Leadbeater, *Personalisation through Participation: A new script for public services* (London: Demos, 2004).

95　C Dustmann and F Fabbri, 'Language proficiency and labour market performance of immigrants in the UK', *Economic Journal* 113, no 489 (July 2003), available at www.res.org.uk/economic/ejtoc.asp?ref=0013-0133&vid=113&iid=489&oc (accessed 25 Feb 2007).

96　The words of Hortance Mbelu's speech are recorded in J Ward, 'Building barriers', *Guardian*, 26 Oct 2006.

97　P Freire, *The Pedagogy of the Oppressed* (Harmondsworth: Penguin, 1986).

98　Lo Bianco, 'Language planning for globalisation tensions and trends'.

99　A de Mesa, 'Branding in tongues', *brandchannel.com*, 27 Nov 2006, available at www.brandchannel.com/start1.asp?fa_id=342 (accessed 26 Feb 2007).

100　A Ardila, 'Spanglish: an anglicised Spanish dialect', *Hispanic Journal of Behavioural Sciences* 27, no 1 (Feb 2005).

101　Gordon Jr (ed), *Ethnologue*.

102　D Cho, '"Koreatown" image divides a changing Annandale', *Washington Post*, 14 May 2005.

103　For further details, see D Montgomery, 'An anthem's discordant notes', *Washington Post*, 28 Apr 2006, available at www.washingtonpost.com/wp-dyn/content/article/2006/04/27/AR2006042702505.html (accessed 26 Feb 2007).

104　See coverage in *USA Today*, www.usatoday.com/life/music/news/2006-04-27-spanish-spangled-banner_x.htm (accessed 6 Nov 2006).

105　A Dorfman, 'America is a bilingual nation', *Guardian*, 10 May 2006.

106　See www.pingwales.co.uk/2006/11/23/Bilingual-services-provision.html (accessed 26 Feb 2007).

107　D Crystal, *English as a Global Language*.

108　See http://news.bbc.co.uk/1/hi/education/6330961.stm (accessed 7 Feb 2007).

109　A Asthana, 'Language crisis facing UK schools', *Observer*, 3 Dec 2006.

110　A Poirier, 'Tongue tied', *Guardian*, 26 Aug 2006.

111　R Garner, 'Europe tells UK: improve teaching of our languages', *Independent*, 11 Feb 2002.

112　R Garner, 'German ambassador criticises UK over failings at languages', *Independent*, 13 Dec 2005.

113 'Government to review language policy', *FE News*, 17 Oct 2006, available at www.fenews.co.uk/newsview.asp?n=1977 (accessed 26 Feb 2007).

114 Eurobarometer, 'Europeans and their languages', Feb 2006, available at http://ec.europa.eu/public_opinion/archives/ebs/ebs_243_sum_en.pdf (accessed 26 Feb 2007).

115 H Footitt, *The National Languages Strategy in Higher Education*, research report RR625 (London: Department for Education and Skills, 2005).

116 E Morris, 'Sorry Alan, it seems I dropped you in it', *Guardian*, 24 Oct 2006.

117 See, for example, Crystal, *English as a Global Language*.

118 Graddol, *English Next*.

119 Ibid.

120 British Chambers of Commerce/London School of Commerce, *The Impact of Foreign Languages on British Business, Qualitative Results* (Nov 2003) and *Quantitative Results* (May 2004) (London: BCC/LSC, 2003, 2004).

121 'International business owners survey' (London: Grant Thornton, 2004), see www.grant-thornton.co.uk (accessed 26 Feb 2007).

122 Federation of Small Businesses, *Biennial Membership Survey* (2004), quoted in National Centre for Languages (CILT), *Talking World Class* (London: CILT, July 2005), available at www.cilt.org.uk/key/talkingworldclass.pdf (accessed 27 Feb 2007).

123 Graddol, *English Next*.

124 D Lepkowska, 'UK under threat as English teaching goes global', *Guardian*, 5 Dec 2006.

125 See B Walraff, 'What global language?', *Atlantic Monthly*, Nov 2002; see also, Graddol, *English Next*.

126 Quoted in Lepkowska, 'UK under threat as English teaching goes global'.

127 For the Foundation for Endangered Languages, and statistics on endangered languages, see www.ogmios.org/manifesto.htm (accessed 26 Feb 2007).

128 R Phillipson, *English-only Europe?* (London: Routledge, 2003).

129 Crystal, *English as a Global Language*.

130 A Burgess, *A Mouthful of Air: Language and languages, especially English* (London: Random House, 1992).

131 Gordon Jr (ed), *Ethnologue*.

132 United Nations, *Declaration on the Rights of Persons Belonging to National or Ethnic, Religious and Linguistic Minorities*, 1992, available at www.unhchr.ch/html/menu3/b/d_minori.htm (accessed 27 Feb 2007).

133 R Phillipson, *Linguistic Imperialism* (Oxford: Oxford University Press, 1992).

134 See www.academie-francaise.fr/role/index.html (accessed 24 Nov 2006); the translation is our own; here is the French original:
Le rayonnement de la langue française est menacé par l'expansion de l'anglais, plus précisément de l'américain, qui tend à envahir les esprits, les écrits, le monde de l'audiovisuel.
Le développement de l'anglais est souvent favorisé par l'irruption des nouvelles techniques, le développement accéléré des sciences, le rapprochement inouï que permettent les médias et les autres moyens de communication, tous facteurs qui

bousculent le vocabulaire traditionnel et imposent à marche rapide l'adoption de nouveaux mots.

135 J Johnson, 'Bangalore hit by English ban in primary schools', *Financial Times Deutschland*, 13 Oct 2006.

136 UK Department for International Development, see www.dfid.gov.uk/ (accessed 28 Feb 2007).

137 His 1997 essay was subsequently developed into a book and published as ES Raymond, *The Cathedral and the Bazaar* (Sebastopol, CA: O'Reilly, 1999).

138 'Dalits exaltation of English Language', available at www.ibnlive.com/news/dalits-exaltation-of-english-language/24988-3.html (accessed 26 Feb 2007).

139 Dalit Freedom Network, see www.dalitnetwork.org/go?/dfn/about/C33/ (accessed 28 Feb 2007).

140 R Phillipson and T Skutnabb-Kangas, 'Englishisation: one dimension of globalisation' in D Graddol and UH Meinhof (eds), 'English in a changing world', *Aila Review* 13 (1999).

141 Lord Watson, 'Spreading the word', *RSA Journal* (Oct 2006).

142 I Basu, '"Native English" is losing its power', *Asia Times*, 15 Sep 2006, available at www.atimes.com/atimes/South_Asia/HI15Df01.html (accessed 26 Feb 2007).

143 Anholt, *Brand America*.

144 A Feely and D Winslow, *Talking Sense: A research study of language skills management in major companies* (London: National Centre for Languages, 2005).

145 Crystal, *English as a Global Language?*.

146 Ibid.

147 N Ferguson, *Empire*.

148 For the Confucius Institutes, see 'China to open more Confucius Institutes in Africa to meet demands', *People's Daily*, 21 Jun 2006, (Xinhua News Agency), see http://english.peopledaily.com.cn/200606/21/eng20060621_275830.html (accessed 26 Feb 2007).

149 J Kurlantzick, *Beijing's Safari: China's move into Africa and its implications for aid, development, and governance* (Washington DC: Carnegie Endowment for International Peace, 2006).

150 See http://pewglobal.org/reports/display.php?ReportID=252 (accessed 26 Feb 2007).

151 H De Burgh, *China: Friend or foe?* (Thriplow, Cambridge: Icon Books, 2006).

152 'Chinese language learning increasingly popular in Africa', *People's Daily*, 7 Nov 2006, available at http://english.people.com.cn/200611/07/ eng20061107_319217.html (accessed 26 Feb 2007).

153 For further details, see P Starr, 'Their sun also rises', *American Prospect*, Apr 2005.

154 E Sidiropoulos, speaking at 'China in Africa: a view from the continent', Chatham House, 25 Sep 2006, available at www.chathamhouse.org.uk/ pdf/meeting_transcripts/250906sidiropoulos.pdf (accessed 26 Feb 2007).

155 D Barboza, 'MTV to put content on "Chinese Google"', *International Herald and Tribune*, 18 Oct 2006.

156 Quoted in J Perlez, 'Chinese move to eclipse US appeal in Southeast Asia', *New York Times*, 18 Nov 2004.

157 See United Nations Conference on Trade and Development, *World Investment Report, 2005: Transnational corporations and the internationalisation of R&D* (Geneva: UNCTAD, 2005), cited in Graddol, *English Next*.

158 These figures are from the British Embassy in Beijing, see www.uk.cn/bj/index.asp?menu_id=379&artid=1138 (accessed 26 Feb 2007).

159 US Census Bureau, *Language Use and English-Speaking Ability: 2000*, Census 2000 Brief, available at www.census.gov/prod/2003pubs/c2kbr-29.pdf (accessed 28 Feb 2007).

160 J Laponce, 'Babel and the market'.

161 C Geertz, *The Interpretation of Cultures* (Oxford: Oxford University Press, 1973).

162 For an analysis of the 'market as a moderator for territorialism', see ibid.

163 See J Wilsdon et al, Atlas of Ideas project, www.demos.co.uk/projects/atlasofideas/overview (accessed 5 Mar 2007).

164 G Mulgan, T Steinberg and O Salem, *Wide Open: Open source methods and their future potential* (London: Demos, 2005).

165 Crystal, *English as a Global Language*.

166 S Poole, *Unspeak* (London: Little Brown, 2006).

167 For further details see www.cultureonline.gov.uk/projects/in_production/webplay/index.html (accessed 26 Feb 2007) and www.webplay.org (accessed 26 Feb 2007).

168 M Mean and C Tims, *People Make Places: Growing the public life of cities* (London: Demos, 2005).

169 For further details see MB Sheridan, 'Va. state police swap "10-4" for "message understood"', *Washington Post*, 13 Nov 2006, available www.washingtonpost.com/wp-dyn/content/article/2006/11/12/AR2006111201098_pf.html (accessed 26 Feb 2007).

170 See 'Chinese language learning increasingly popular in Africa'.

171 Quoted from an interview on Chicago's *Worldview* Radio show, 12 Sep 2006.

172 P Jain and G Groot, 'Beijing's "soft power" offensive', *Asia Times*, 17 May 2006.

173 Interview with Demos researcher, 17 Oct 2006.

174 M Erard, 'Saying "global" in Chinese', *Foreign Policy*, May/June 2006.

175 Ibid.

176 See, for example, 'Schools "must teach Britishness"', BBC News, 25 Jan 2007, available at http://news.bbc.co.uk/1/hi/education/6294643.stm (accessed 26 Feb 2007).

177 SP Huntingdon, 'The clash of civilizations?', *Foreign Affairs*, Summer 1993, available at www.foreignaffairs.org/19930601FAESSAY5188-faarticles/samuel-p-huntington/the-clash-of-civilizations.html (accessed 28 Feb 2007).

178 B Seidlhofer, 'Research perspectives on teaching English as a lingua franca',

Annual Review of Applied Linguistics 24 (2004).

179 J Jenkins, 'Points of view and blind spots: ELF and SLA', *International Journal of Applied Linguistics* 16, no 2 (2006).

180 Ibid, citing H Babha, *The Location of Culture* (London: Routledge, 1994); C Kramsch, *Context and Culture in Language Teaching* (Oxford: Oxford University Press, 1993); and C Kramsch, 'Language study as border study: experiencing difference', *European Journal of Education* 8, no 2 (1993).

181 C Leadbeater and J Wilsdon, *The Atlas of Ideas: How Asian innovation can benefit us all* (London: Demos, 2007).

182 C Tims, *The Biggest Learning Opportunity on Earth: How London's Olympics could work for young people in schools* (London: Demos, 2007).

183 Quoted in Warschauer, 'Languages.com'.

DEMOS – Licence to Publish

THE WORK (AS DEFINED BELOW) IS PROVIDED UNDER THE TERMS OF THIS LICENCE ("LICENCE"). THE WORK IS PROTECTED BY COPYRIGHT AND/OR OTHER APPLICABLE LAW. ANY USE OF THE WORK OTHER THAN AS AUTHORIZED UNDER THIS LICENCE IS PROHIBITED. BY EXERCISING ANY RIGHTS TO THE WORK PROVIDED HERE, YOU ACCEPT AND AGREE TO BE BOUND BY THE TERMS OF THIS LICENCE. DEMOS GRANTS YOU THE RIGHTS CONTAINED HERE IN CONSIDERATION OF YOUR ACCEPTANCE OF SUCH TERMS AND CONDITIONS.

1. **Definitions**
   a **"Collective Work"** means a work, such as a periodical issue, anthology or encyclopedia, in which the Work in its entirety in unmodified form, along with a number of other contributions, constituting separate and independent works in themselves, are assembled into a collective whole. A work that constitutes a Collective Work will not be considered a Derivative Work (as defined below) for the purposes of this Licence.
   b **"Derivative Work"** means a work based upon the Work or upon the Work and other pre-existing works, such as a musical arrangement, dramatization, fictionalization, motion picture version, sound recording, art reproduction, abridgment, condensation, or any other form in which the Work may be recast, transformed, or adapted, except that a work that constitutes a Collective Work or a translation from English into another language will not be considered a Derivative Work for the purpose of this Licence.
   c **"Licensor"** means the individual or entity that offers the Work under the terms of this Licence.
   d **"Original Author"** means the individual or entity who created the Work.
   e **"Work"** means the copyrightable work of authorship offered under the terms of this Licence.
   f **"You"** means an individual or entity exercising rights under this Licence who has not previously violated the terms of this Licence with respect to the Work, or who has received express permission from DEMOS to exercise rights under this Licence despite a previous violation.
2. **Fair Use Rights.** Nothing in this licence is intended to reduce, limit, or restrict any rights arising from fair use, first sale or other limitations on the exclusive rights of the copyright owner under copyright law or other applicable laws.
3. **Licence Grant.** Subject to the terms and conditions of this Licence, Licensor hereby grants You a worldwide, royalty-free, non-exclusive, perpetual (for the duration of the applicable copyright) licence to exercise the rights in the Work as stated below:
   a to reproduce the Work, to incorporate the Work into one or more Collective Works, and to reproduce the Work as incorporated in the Collective Works;
   b to distribute copies or phonorecords of, display publicly, perform publicly, and perform publicly by means of a digital audio transmission the Work including as incorporated in Collective Works;
   The above rights may be exercised in all media and formats whether now known or hereafter devised. The above rights include the right to make such modifications as are technically necessary to exercise the rights in other media and formats. All rights not expressly granted by Licensor are hereby reserved.
4. **Restrictions.** The licence granted in Section 3 above is expressly made subject to and limited by the following restrictions:
   a You may distribute, publicly display, publicly perform, or publicly digitally perform the Work only under the terms of this Licence, and You must include a copy of, or the Uniform Resource Identifier for, this Licence with every copy or phonorecord of the Work You distribute, publicly display, publicly perform, or publicly digitally perform. You may not offer or impose any terms on the Work that alter or restrict the terms of this Licence or the recipients' exercise of the rights granted hereunder. You may not sublicense the Work. You must keep intact all notices that refer to this Licence and to the disclaimer of warranties. You may not distribute, publicly display, publicly perform, or publicly digitally perform the Work with any technological measures that control access or use of the Work in a manner inconsistent with the terms of this Licence Agreement. The above applies to the Work as incorporated in a Collective Work, but this does not require the Collective Work apart from the Work itself to be made subject to the terms of this Licence. If You create a Collective Work, upon notice from any Licencor You must, to the extent practicable, remove from the Collective Work any reference to such Licensor or the Original Author, as requested.
   b You may not exercise any of the rights granted to You in Section 3 above in any manner that is primarily intended for or directed toward commercial advantage or private monetary

compensation. The exchange of the Work for other copyrighted works by means of digital file-sharing or otherwise shall not be considered to be intended for or directed toward commercial advantage or private monetary compensation, provided there is no payment of any monetary compensation in connection with the exchange of copyrighted works.

c If you distribute, publicly display, publicly perform, or publicly digitally perform the Work or any Collective Works, You must keep intact all copyright notices for the Work and give the Original Author credit reasonable to the medium or means You are utilizing by conveying the name (or pseudonym if applicable) of the Original Author if supplied; the title of the Work if supplied. Such credit may be implemented in any reasonable manner; provided, however, that in the case of a Collective Work, at a minimum such credit will appear where any other comparable authorship credit appears and in a manner at least as prominent as such other comparable authorship credit.

5. Representations, Warranties and Disclaimer

a By offering the Work for public release under this Licence, Licensor represents and warrants that, to the best of Licensor's knowledge after reasonable inquiry:

  i Licensor has secured all rights in the Work necessary to grant the licence rights hereunder and to permit the lawful exercise of the rights granted hereunder without You having any obligation to pay any royalties, compulsory licence fees, residuals or any other payments;

  ii The Work does not infringe the copyright, trademark, publicity rights, common law rights or any other right of any third party or constitute defamation, invasion of privacy or other tortious injury to any third party.

b EXCEPT AS EXPRESSLY STATED IN THIS LICENCE OR OTHERWISE AGREED IN WRITING OR REQUIRED BY APPLICABLE LAW, THE WORK IS LICENCED ON AN "AS IS" BASIS, WITHOUT WARRANTIES OF ANY KIND, EITHER EXPRESS OR IMPLIED INCLUDING, WITHOUT LIMITATION, ANY WARRANTIES REGARDING THE CONTENTS OR ACCURACY OF THE WORK.

6. Limitation on Liability. EXCEPT TO THE EXTENT REQUIRED BY APPLICABLE LAW, AND EXCEPT FOR DAMAGES ARISING FROM LIABILITY TO A THIRD PARTY RESULTING FROM BREACH OF THE WARRANTIES IN SECTION 5, IN NO EVENT WILL LICENSOR BE LIABLE TO YOU ON ANY LEGAL THEORY FOR ANY SPECIAL, INCIDENTAL, CONSEQUENTIAL, PUNITIVE OR EXEMPLARY DAMAGES ARISING OUT OF THIS LICENCE OR THE USE OF THE WORK, EVEN IF LICENSOR HAS BEEN ADVISED OF THE POSSIBILITY OF SUCH DAMAGES.

7. Termination

a This Licence and the rights granted hereunder will terminate automatically upon any breach by You of the terms of this Licence. Individuals or entities who have received Collective Works from You under this Licence, however, will not have their licences terminated provided such individuals or entities remain in full compliance with those licences. Sections 1, 2, 5, 6, 7, and 8 will survive any termination of this Licence.

b Subject to the above terms and conditions, the licence granted here is perpetual (for the duration of the applicable copyright in the Work). Notwithstanding the above, Licensor reserves the right to release the Work under different licence terms or to stop distributing the Work at any time; provided, however that any such election will not serve to withdraw this Licence (or any other licence that has been, or is required to be, granted under the terms of this Licence), and this Licence will continue in full force and effect unless terminated as stated above.

8. Miscellaneous

a Each time You distribute or publicly digitally perform the Work or a Collective Work, DEMOS offers to the recipient a licence to the Work on the same terms and conditions as the licence granted to You under this Licence.

b If any provision of this Licence is invalid or unenforceable under applicable law, it shall not affect the validity or enforceability of the remainder of the terms of this Licence, and without further action by the parties to this agreement, such provision shall be reformed to the minimum extent necessary to make such provision valid and enforceable.

c No term or provision of this Licence shall be deemed waived and no breach consented to unless such waiver or consent shall be in writing and signed by the party to be charged with such waiver or consent.

d This Licence constitutes the entire agreement between the parties with respect to the Work licensed here. There are no understandings, agreements or representations with respect to the Work not specified here. Licensor shall not be bound by any additional provisions that may appear in any communication from You. This Licence may not be modified without the mutual written agreement of DEMOS and You.